W9-BMV-277

Drinks for All Ages

The Original Guide to Alcohol-Free Beverages and Drinks

Robert Plotkin

BarMedia
Tucson, Arizona
©2002

This book is dedicated to my daughters
— Sarah Joelle and Hannah Marie —
for a bunch of really good reasons,
not the least of which is laughing at my jokes
and allowing me to be a part of your daily life.
RP

Other Books by Robert Plotkin

The Professional Bartender's Training Manual — 3rd Edition (2002)
The Bartender's Companion: The Original Guide to American Cocktails and Drinks — 4th Edition (2001)
Caribe Rum: The Original Guide to Caribbean Rum and Drinks (2001)
Successful Beverage Management: Proven Strategies for the On-Premise Operator (2000)
¡Toma! Margaritas! The Original Guide to Margaritas and Tequila (1999)
Preventing Internal Theft: A Bar Owner's Guide — 2nd Edition (1998)
Increasing Bar Sales: Creative Twists to Bigger Profits (1997)
Reducing Bar Costs: A Survival Guide for the '90s (1993)
501 Questions Every Bartender Should Know How to Answer: A Unique Look at the Bar Business (1993)
The Professional Guide to Bartending: An Encyclopedia of American Mixology (1991)
The Intervention Handbook: The Legal Aspects of Serving Alcohol — 2nd Edition (1990)

Publishers:	Carol Plotkin, Robert Plotkin
Editors:	Sheila Berry, Miguel Castillo, Karen Schmidt
Managing Editor:	Robert Plotkin
Production Manager:	Carol Plotkin
Cover Design:	Miguel Castillo, Carol Plotkin
Book Design:	Miguel Castillo

Published by: **BarMedia**

P.O. Box 14486
Tucson, AZ 85732
520.747.8131
www.BarMedia.com

The TABASCO® marks, bottle and label designs are registered trademarks and servicemarks exclusively of McIlhenny Co., Avery Island, LA 70513.

Copyright 2002 BarMedia

All rights reserved. No part of this book may be reproduced or transmitted in any form or by any means, electronic or mechanical, including photocopying, recording, or by any information storage or retrieval system, without written permission from the publisher, except by a reviewer who may quote brief passages. The information in this book is true and correct to the best of our knowledge. It is offered with no guarantees on the part of the authors or BarMedia. The authors and BarMedia disclaim all liability in connection with the use of this book.

ISBN: 0-945562-29-2

Printed in China
First Printing

Table of Contents

Acknowledgements iii

Introduction iv

Chapter 1: Alcohol-Free Versions of America's Favorite Cocktails 1
    Here's an opportunity to make delicious classic cocktails, all without
    a drop of alcohol.

Chapter 2: Alcohol-Free Marys, Caesars and Sangritas 13
    Serve exuberant libations with no possibility of causing a hangover.

Chapter 3: Ice Cream Drinks Appeal to the Kid in All of Us 23
    Tempt guests with irresistible, dessert-like ice cream specialties.
    It's a "can't miss" proposition.

Chapter 4: Smoothies Break into the Popular Mainstream 29
    Smoothies are delicious alternatives to fast food lunches and
    empty-calorie snacks.

Chapter 5: Kid's Drinks! Making the Grade with Minor Leaguers 37
    "Special" to kids means a fun, great tasting drink that mom and dad
    don't usually let them drink at home.

Chapter 6: Specialty Products and the Sizzle They Add to Drinks 43
    Items to rim with, flavor with, add color and pizzazz, are but a few of
    the invaluable products used in the drink making process.

Chapter 7: No Longer 5¢ a Glass, Lemonade has Gone Uptown 49
    Refreshing, tall and thirst quenching, lemonade is no longer restricted to
    spring and summer. Discover many variations on this American classic.

Chapter 8: Popping the Top Off the World of Sodas 55

Sodas are effervescent, flavorful and is a big part of American life. Find out what's out there besides the Root Beer Float.

Chapter 9: Effervescent or Not, Apple Cider is Pressed for Success 61

Chilled, bubbly, warmed and mulled, apple cider is a great American beverage with a great diversity of uses.

Chapter 10: Juices Grab Their Share of the Limelight 65

Discover why professional mixologists and social hosts alike have found juices invaluable in creating alcohol-free specialties.

Chapter 11: Exploring America's Love Affair with Coffee 69

There is no other beverage more ingrained in the average American's daily life than coffee. Here's a host of fascinating coffee combinations to keep one amused.

Chapter 12: Making the Most of Cocoa Drinks 85

Great alcohol-free specialties made with hot cocoa have a high likelihood of generating a standing ovation.

Chapter 13: Tea Time is Any Time 91

Whether served hot or over ice, enjoy a variety of tastes and types in these delicious specialty drinks.

Chapter 14: Showcasing Your Drinks in Specialty Glassware................99

Use glassware that is as special as what is going inside. View scores of creative glassware options.

Index 101

Resources 105

Acknowledgements

Perhaps more than any other book BarMedia has produced, *Drinks For All Ages: The Original Guide to Alcohol-Free Beverages and Drinks* was a collaborative effort. To fulfill its mission, I tapped the knowledge and creative talents of many individuals, all of whom I want to recognize at this time.

To produce this book, I sought out information from many different sources. Many people graciously shared their knowledge and provided insights into their specific areas of expertise. Without their assistance this book would be severely lacking.

While my name may be on the cover, many people worked long and hard to create this book. I want to thank Karen Schmidt and Sheila Berry for their endless encouragement and editing prowess. And a special thanks to Elisa Carrizoza for her special brand of inspiration.

I also need to thank Miguel Castillo. He was responsible for designing the book's cover and interior layout, however, his sound judgement, unfathomable talents and devotion to excellence were also invaluable to this project.

Last, I want to express my heartfelt gratitude and admiration to my wife and partner, Carol Plotkin, for her innumerable contributions, all the while being the role model for our two daughters.

Introduction

There is a world of choices for people who entertain with alcohol. But what fun awaits people who don't drink alcohol? They are in the majority, after all. What options do they have when it comes to what to drink when out on the town or at a social function? The answers lie between the covers of this book.

While it's likely that some in the food and beverage industry have long appreciated the importance of alcohol-free beverages and drinks, I was not among them. After spending most of my life preparing untold numbers of alcohol-laced cocktails, I may have been a bit slow to perceive the needs of non-imbibers. I trust that I am not alone in this. But for the past 4 or 5 years, I've seen the light and what a bright light it is.

After all, who said a cocktail had to have a kick to be something special? Isn't it possible to make a great tasting, great looking drink without adding a drop of alcohol? Absolutely and this book will prove it.

If you're in the hospitality business and you need some financial incentive before jumping on board, consider the magnitude of this untapped market. The demographics of alcohol-free drinkers include literally everyone. Consider also that alcohol-free beverages and drinks are loaded with profit. Add in that these libations can be served without incurring civil liability and you'll begin to get the picture.

If you're a social host, conventions are changing. There are occasions where serving alcohol isn't appropriate, but your guests still deserve to sip something fabulous. So while you're dreaming up your party strategies, don't forget to factor in some creative alcohol-free ideas. Your guests will appreciate it.

To all parties concerned, I would like to offer this one, all-important insight. It is regrettable that the term "non-alcoholic" has become a standard phrase within our industry. Non-alcoholic suggests that there is something integral missing from a beverage or drink. Says who? The same can be said for menu headers such as "mocktails," "faux-tinis" and "truncated cocktails." These labels only serve to demean the product and the person ordering it.

The name applied to these beverages and drinks is "alcohol-free." You don't need to add alcohol to excel at drink making. It's a positive phrase for a positive subject.

So go ahead and serve your guests a thick, rich milkshake, a tall glass of bubble tea, or perhaps a raspberry-flavored lemonade. Maybe they'd rather sip on a caffé latte or mug of hot cocoa with a scoop of French vanilla ice cream. Whatever their personal preferences may be, the creative ideas captured in this book will keep your guests enthralled for years to come.

Robert Plotkin
BarMedia
Tucson, Arizona
2002

Chapter 1

Alcohol-Free Versions of America's Favorite Cocktails

Who said a great cocktail had to contain alcohol? There are growing legions of people who are looking to entertain and be entertained without it. For many, it's a matter of enjoying the taste of a cocktail without any of the potential side effects.

Creating alcohol-free cocktails involves as much art and skill as does mixing with spirited ingredients. There are scores of interesting and high quality products that can be used in their creation. More importantly, alcohol-free cocktails are every bit as delicious and worthy of public acclaim as any that are spiked with spirits.

So is it possible to create hangover-free versions of some of America's favorite cocktails? Absolutely, provided one selects the right drinks to feature. Classics such as the martini, old fashion, or Manhattan are liquor driven recipes, therefore dropping them out of consideration. Other concoctions that essentially disqualify themselves are the whiskey sour, mint julep, kamikaze and cosmopolitan. The spirit bases in these recipes are integral to achieving the desired flavor profile. Simple highball combinations, such as the screwdriver or gin & tonic, exist only in the spirit world and are best left alone.

Nearly every other classic recipe can be recreated in an alcohol-free version. This chapter is loaded with creative variations on traditional themes, such as alcohol-free, daiquiris, margaritas, piña coladas and sangrias. The only thing to watch out for with these hangover-free drinks are the calories, as if that's really a concern.

Creating Alcohol-Free Classics

The enduring popularity of these recipes suggests there is something timeless about the way they taste. For example, the grasshopper is a famed drink that marries the flavors of mint (crème de menthe), chocolate (crème de cacao) and ice cream together. Add some Torani Chocolate Mint Syrup to a few scoops of ice cream and the resulting concoction will be a dead ringer to the conventionally prepared version.

The following explores how to recreate the character and personality of the major players in the world of mixology without adding a drop of alcohol.

Daiquiris — The daiquiri originated in Cuba in the 1920s, when Cuba was renowned for having the most capable, professional bartenders in the world. It is one of the drinks made famous by Ernest Hemingway and was President Kennedy's drink of choice.

The daiquiri is one of the quintessential cocktails, perfectly balanced between sweet and tart, and loaded with flavor. The original daiquiri was made with light rum, fresh lime juice and sugar. It was then shaken and strained into a chilled cocktail glass.

Alcohol-free daiquiris can be made with a bevy of different products. It is an ideal drink in which to feature exotic fruits such as guava, mango and papaya. Daiquiris can be made with ice cream or sherbet, and are often flavored with coconut, banana, strawberry, raspberry and passion fruit.

Margaritas — The margarita has become the most popular specialty drink in the country. While a large part of its character is predicated on the use of tequila, there are numerous creative ways of preparing delicious margaritas that do not use tequila.

The basic construction of an alcohol-free margarita requires sweetened lemon juice (sweet 'n' sour), fresh lime juice and a dose of orange juice. Shake the mixture, or blend with ice, and serve in a specialty glass with a salted rim. The resulting concoction is refreshing and exceptionally easy to drink.

Like the piña colada, the margarita is an adaptable recipe and can accommodate many different complementary flavors. As the recipes in this chapter prove, there are alcohol-free specialty margaritas made with fruits of every description, as well as peppers, iced tea, prickly pear cactus, cider, pepper sauce, salsa, sorbet and ice cream.

Piña Coladas — This classic drink is an excellent candidate for promotion to the ranks of alcohol-free. In a well-made piña colada, the flavor of coconut and pineapple dance rings around the subtle taste of light rum, which in some instances, adds little taste to the drink.

One of the piña colada's most marketable attributes is its versatility. The blended drink's pineapple and coconut base marries well with other flavors. For example, a shot of coffee or chocolate is a welcome addition to its overall flavor. Piña coladas also taste great with melon, banana, orange, strawberries, raspberries, lemon, or vanilla.

Since the piña colada is intended to be a sublime tropical experience, one trick of the trade is to blend the drink with ice cream. The result is a thicker, more flavorful concoction. This tactic allows a new avenue of creative thought, for in addition to vanilla ice cream, optional flavors to consider are chocolate, French vanilla, banana, strawberry and coffee. Of course, one could argue that there are at least 31 flavors from which to choose.

Sangrias — In Spain and throughout Europe the prescribed remedy for beating the heat is sangria, a beautiful marriage of fruit juice and wine. Alcohol-free sangrias are a marvelous way to quench a thirst. They are easily prepared on a base of various fruit juices, flavored syrups and handfuls of sliced fruit. For best results, sangrias should be made by the pitcher and allowed to fully steep several hours prior to service. They're not quickly prepared, but are well worth the wait.

CANDIED LEMON DROP

House specialty glass, ice
Rim glass with Franco's
    Lemon Drop Sugar
Pour ingredients into iced mixing glass
1 oz. vanilla syrup
1 oz. ReaLemon Lemon Juice
6 oz. pineapple juice
Shake and strain
Splash club soda
Lemon twist for garnish

DAIQUIRI, BOGUS BANANA

House specialty glass, chilled
Rim glass with sugar
Pour ingredients into blender
1 oz. Torani Butter Rum Syrup
3 oz. True Crystals Banana Daiquiri Mix
1/2 oz. fresh lime juice
3 oz. sweet 'n' sour
Blend ingredients with ice
Orange wheel and banana slice garnish

DAIQUIRI, BONUSBERRY

House specialty glass, chilled
Rim glass with Franco's
    Raspberry-Flavored Sugar
Pour ingredients into blender
1/2 cup raspberries or strawberries
3 oz. Mr & Mrs T Strawberry
    Daiquiri-Margarita Mix
1 oz. blueberry syrup
1/2 oz. Rose's Lime Juice
2 oz. sweet 'n' sour
Blend ingredients with ice
Drizzle raspberry syrup
Strawberry garnish

DAIQUIRI, COCO-NONRUM

House specialty glass, ice
*Pour ingredients into
    iced mixing glass*
2 oz. Coco López
    Cream of Coconut
1/2 oz. fresh lime juice
5 oz. sweet 'n' sour
Shake and strain
Lime wedge garnish

MARGARITAVILLE® MARGARITA MIX

Parrot heads now have reason to rejoice. Jimmy Buffet and Mott's have created a mix that captures the dreamy state of perpetual relaxation that has come to be known as Margaritaville. Appropriately dubbed MARGARITAVILLE MARGARITA MIX, everything about this elixir is reminiscent of the Florida Keys, seaside sunsets and languid evenings sipping frozen concoctions from a blender.

Alcohol-free Margaritaville Margarita Mix has the look of freshly squeezed lime juice and a subtle yet pleasant citrus bouquet. It is light-bodied with a classic sweet and sour palate where neither quality dominates. The finish is clean, moderately tart and long lasting. The mix is refreshing poured over ice directly from the bottle.

For an alcohol-free Margaritaville Margarita, add in a healthy splash of orange juice, perhaps some grapefruit juice, then shake well and serve with ice and a lime wedge garnish in a salt rimmed glass. Another option is to blend the ingredients with ice into a slushy margarita. There are also scores of creative variations, such as a hangover-free strawberry or raspberry margarita.

There's no reason on Earth to typecast this fine mix and relegate it to alcohol-free margarita duty only. Because the Margaritaville mix has a traditional lemon-lime constitution, it can be recruited for use in making alcohol-free daiquiris. For example, a variation on the banana daiquiri theme requires a whole ripe banana, a scoop or two of vanilla ice cream, a small dose of vanilla extract and Margaritaville mix as the base. Blend the ingredients and let the kudos roll in.

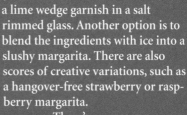

MAJOR PETERS' PIÑA COLADA COCKTAIL MIX

Following the success of Major Peters' Bloody Mary, the company launched a line of premium cocktail mixes that has since become a mainstay in many of the big names in restaurants and hotels. It's guaranteed that if professional mixologists rely on a mix, it has paid its dues.

Alcohol-free MAJOR PETERS' PIÑA COLADA COCKTAIL MIX spearheads the successful line. It eliminates all of the guesswork and hassle behind building a specialty colada. The mix has the color of fresh coconut, a soft citrus bouquet and the flavor is a sublime marriage of pineapple and coconut. The marvelously thick consistency makes it an ideal base for a tall, blended drink. As for ease of use, just pour and blend away.

The Major Peters' Strawberry Daiquiri/Margarita Cocktail Mix is well suited for its intended use. The flavor has an authentic, freshly picked quality, and a palate that's decidedly more tart than sweet. The true-to-life, strawberry red color of the mix is another marketable attribute.

Tailor-made for use in alcohol-free cocktails, the Major Peters' Margarita Cocktail Mix is a balanced offering of lemon and lime flavors with prominent notes of orange. It is particularly tart, with just the right hint of sweetness and mixes well with a wide array of other flavors. The aromatic mix is highly versatile and has unlimited creative possibilities.

Major Peters' Grenadine is delectably rich and brimming with the flavor of pomegranates, while the company's sweetened lime juice has a tart and refreshing palate and a squeaky clean finish.

DAIQUIRI, FAUX FLORIDA
House specialty glass, ice
Pour ingredients into iced mixing glass
2 oz. True Crystals
    Raspberry Daiquiri Mix
1/4 oz. Rose's Grenadine
1/2 oz. Rose's Lime Juice
1 oz. fresh lime juice
1 1/2 oz. grapefruit juice
1 1/2 oz. sweet 'n' sour
Shake and strain
Lime wedge garnish

DAIQUIRI, FAUX STRAWBERRY
House specialty glass, chilled
Rim glass with Franco's
    Lemon Drop Sugar
Pour ingredients into blender
2 oz. strawberry puree
1 oz. ReaLime Lime Juice
4 oz. sweet 'n' sour
Blend ingredients with ice
Sugar dipped strawberry garnish

DAIQUIRI, MOCK VANILLA
House specialty glass, chilled
Pour ingredients into blender
1 oz. Torani Ginger Spice Syrup
1 oz. Torani Vanilla Syrup
1 oz. half & half cream
4 oz. sweet 'n' sour
Blend ingredients with ice
Whipped cream and drizzle Torani
    Almond Roca® Syrup garnish

DAIQUIRI, PLACID
House specialty glass, ice
Rim glass with Franco's
    Cherry-Flavored Sugar
*Pour ingredients into
    iced mixing glass*
1 oz. Torani Pink
    Grapefruit Syrup
1/2 oz. Rose's Lime Juice
2 oz. passion fruit juice
4 oz. Freshies Peach-Mango
    Margarita Mix
Shake and strain
Orange twist garnish

DAIQUIRI, RIGHTEOUS PIÑA

House specialty glass, chilled
Pour ingredients into blender
1 1/2 oz. pineapple syrup
2-3 pineapple slices, cored and peeled
1/2 oz. fresh lime juice
3 oz. sweet 'n' sour
Blend ingredients with ice
Orange wheel, pineapple wedge
    and cherry garnish

DAIQUIRI, SAINT HEMINGWAY

House specialty glass, ice
Pour ingredients into iced mixing glass
3/4 oz. maraschino cherry juice
1 oz. grapefruit juice
1 oz. ReaLime Lime Juice
1/2 oz. Rose's Lime Juice
4 oz. sweet 'n' sour
Shake and strain
Lime wheel garnish

DAIQUIRI, UNPRICKLY PEAR

House specialty glass, ice
Rim glass with red-colored sugar
Pour ingredients into iced mixing glass
1 oz. lemon syrup
1 oz. fresh lime juice
2 oz. prickly pear puree
4 oz. sweet 'n' sour
Shake and strain
Lime wedge garnish

DAIQUIRI, VIRGIN MINT

House specialty glass, chilled
Rim glass with sugar
Pour ingredients into blender
1 oz. Torani Mandarin
    Orange Syrup
3/4 oz. Torani
    Crème de Menthe Syrup
2 mint leaves
1/2 oz. fresh lime juice
4 oz. sweet 'n' sour
Blend ingredients with ice
Mint sprig garnish

DR. SWAMI & BONE DADDY'S TOP SHELF MARGARITA MIX

The only mystery about this product is who the heck are Dr. Swami and Bone Daddy? Other than that, everything else is perfectly clear. This line of gourmet mixes originated in Northern California where it quickly gained a popular following. One thing naturally followed another and soon the line of small batch mixes had become famous.

DR. SWAMI & BONE DADDY'S TOP SHELF MARGARITA MIX is a delicious, high quality product made from tree-ripened limes and lemons, and sugar cane as a sweetener. In a masterful stroke of genius, the good doctor and Bone Daddy splashed in a dose of grapefruit juice for an intriguing and unexpected burst of flavor. This is a mix that was created for more than just margaritas.

While this is indeed a top shelf mix, remember the adage about buying quality and never being disappointed. The mix is endowed with excellent color, a citrus bouquet and a light, smooth body with a small amount of pulp for good measure. The lemon-lime palate is lively, flavorful and appropriately tart on the finish. It's a creative boost to any alcohol-free repertoire.

The line also includes Dr. Swami & Bone Daddy's Gourmet Bloody Mary Mix. Featuring the likes of Lea & Perrins Worcestershire sauce, horseradish and TABASCO® Pepper Sauce, it is ideally balanced with no one flavor dominating the palate.

Dr. Swami & Bone Daddy's Piña Colada Mix is an alcohol-free gem, made with pineapple juice and shredded coconut. It's delectably thick, rich and is ready to use at a moments notice.

TRUE CRYSTALS® SANGRIA MIXER

Sangria was born in the villages of Spain, where it remains a national treasure. The drink traditionally is prepared by the pitcher with dry red wine and a lavish assortment of juices and fresh fruit. With or without the wine, well-made sangria is a thing of joy and about as easy to drink as anything served in a glass. No thirst can withstand it. Like most great works of art, however, the sangria takes time to create.

With TRUE CRYSTALS® SANGRIA MIXER, it only takes a minute to begin unraveling the mysteries of this punch-like concoction. The mixer is made from a blend of fresh lime, lemon and orange juices, and sweetened for balance. The juices are freeze-dried using patented technology to capture the pure, natural flavor of the fruit. Add water and a minute later the mixer is ready to serve.

The True Crystals® Sangria Mixer has a ruby red appearance and a fruit laced bouquet. The mixer is medium-bodied with a lush texture and a full, fruity palate with a robust, bright taste. The flavor immediately fills the mouth, followed shortly by a wave of cheek puckering tartness. The tangy and flavorful finish is long lasting.

The creative potential for this product is boundless. For example, use the Sangria Mixer as a base, pour in some True Crystals® Peach Daiquiri Mixer and Raspberry Daiquiri Mixer, then serve over ice with a mound of sliced limes, lemons and oranges. An optional splash of seltzer or lemon-lime soda adds an invigorating spritz to the drink.

FILAPIÑA, THE
House specialty glass, ice
Pour ingredients into iced mixing glass
1 oz. peach syrup
1 oz. passion fruit syrup
1 oz. grapefruit juice
2 oz. pineapple juice
2 oz. sweet 'n' sour
Shake and strain
Fill with club soda
Pineapple wedge garnish

HEALTHIE ZOMBIE
House specialty glass, ice
Rim glass with Franco's
    Lemon Drop Sugar
Pour ingredients into iced mixing glass
1 oz. passion fruit syrup
1/2 oz. vanilla syrup
1/2 oz. Rose's Lime Juice
3 oz. pineapple juice
3 oz. orange juice
Shake and strain
Splash club soda
Float 1/2 oz. grenadine
Lime wedge garnish

HOLY FUZZY NAVEL
House specialty glass, ice
Build in glass
1 oz. peach syrup
Near fill with orange juice
Splash club soda
Orange wheel garnish

IMITATION PLANTER'S PUNCH (1)
House specialty
    glass, ice
*Pour ingredients into
    iced mixing glass*
1 oz. Torani
    Butter Rum Syrup
4 oz. orange juice
4 oz. sweet 'n' sour
1/2 oz. grenadine
2 dashes bitters
Shake and strain
Orange wheel garnish

IMITATION PLANTER'S PUNCH (2)

House specialty glass, ice
Pour ingredients into iced mixing glass
1 oz. vanilla syrup
2 oz. orange juice
2 oz. sweet 'n' sour
1/2 oz. Rose's Grenadine
1 oz. ReaLemon Lemon Juice
2 oz. Mauna La'i Island Guava Juice
Shake and strain
Orange wheel and cherry garnish

IMITATION PLANTER'S PUNCH (3)

House specialty glass, ice
Pour ingredients into iced mixing glass
1 oz. Torani Butter Rum Syrup
3/4 oz. Torani Mandarin Orange Syrup
1 1/2 oz. orange juice
1 1/2 oz. pineapple juice
1 1/2 oz. grapefruit juice
1/2 oz. Rose's Lime Juice
2 dashes bitters
Shake and strain
Orange wheel and cherry garnish

LEMON DROP TEASE

House specialty glass, ice
Rim glass with Franco's
    Lemon Drop Sugar
*Pour ingredients into
    iced mixing glass*
1 oz. lemon syrup
1/2 oz. fresh lemon juice
5 oz. prepared lemonade
Shake and strain
Fill with club soda
Lemon wedge garnish

MAIDEN MADRAS

Highball glass, ice
Build in glass
3 oz. cranberry juice
1 oz. orange juice
Near fill with club soda
Float 1 oz. Torani Mandarin
    Orange Syrup
Orange wheel garnish

FRESHIES PEACH-MANGO MARGARITA MIX

The Freshies company was founded by a chef and a bartender in Telluride, Colorado whose drink mixes became so popular that sharing them with the rest of the world was the only logical next step. Thank goodness that they did. The firm prides itself on not adding artificial colors or preservatives in the products. The quality of their drink mixes is immediately evident.

Under the heading of why leave well enough alone, FRESHIES PEACH-MANGO MARGARITA MIX is a splendid variation on the standard margarita theme. It has a tropical fruit appearance and a voluptuous body. The mix is highly aromatic and crafted to deliver the brilliant ripe flavors of peach and mango simultaneously. The finish is long, tart and full of savory citrus flavor.

The flagship of the line is the original Freshies Fresh Lime Margarita Mix, a fabulously smooth concoction made with freshly squeezed lime and lemon juice. While orange juice and agave nectar are added to tame it some, the mix still has a delightful pucker. The zesty flavor of lime and lemon share equal billing, which is ideal for making alcohol-free margaritas. It is lightly aromatic, medium-bodied and skillfully made. The mix is a refreshing treat on its own.

The boutique line also features Freshies Strawberry-Kiwi Margarita Mix. The initial burst of strawberry flavor is a marvelous counterpoint to the tang of the lime and lemon. The exotic taste of kiwi rounds out the long lasting finish. Like its sisters, the mix has a good color and foams well when shaken.

There are scores of creative uses for these three alcohol-free gems from Freshies.

TRUE CRYSTALS®
RASPBERRY DAIQUIRI MIXER

In a perfect world, raspberries would be in season year round and keep for more than a day or two. As it is, the prized fruit is delicate, highly perishable and available fresh only a few months a year. Nowhere is there a better way to be creative with raspberries behind the bar than with alcohol-free TRUE CRYSTALS® RASPBERRY DAIQUIRI MIXER.

The innovative mixer is made from sun-ripened raspberries and naturally sweetened lime juice. The blend is freeze-dried using patented technology to capture the fresh essence of the fruit. The resulting granules return to their original state with the addition of water. Preparation takes all of a minute.

This True Crystals® mixer has the look, taste and aroma of pureed fresh raspberries. Its irresistible texture and flavor can transform even the most conventional of alcohol-free drinks into something extraordinary. All of the mixers in this line are equally amazing.

The most authentic way to make a kiwi-flavored concoction is with True Crystals® Kiwi Daiquiri Mixer. The same can be said about their banana, mango and peach mixers. They're each made from fresh, ripe fruit and packaged to yield a quart of ready-to-use puree.

The True Crystals® Piña Colada Mixer is made from a blend of coconut macaroon and freeze-dried pineapple juice. Add some water and give a few shakes and it transforms into a luscious, exotic treat. The company also makes an alcohol-free Rum Runner and Tropical Hurricane® Mixer that are sumptuous representations of the popular classics.

MAKE-BELIEVE MAI TAI
House specialty glass, ice
Pour ingredients into iced mixing glass
1/2 oz. lime syrup
2 oz. pineapple juice
3 oz. orange juice
Shake and strain
Near fill with club soda
Float 1/2 oz. orgeat (almond) syrup
Orange wheel garnish

MARGARITA, ANGELIC MELON
House specialty glass, chilled
Rim glass with gold-colored salt
Pour ingredients into blender
1 oz. Torani Watermelon Syrup
1/2 oz. Rose's Lime Juice
1/2 cup honeydew melon, diced
4 oz. True Crystals Margarita Mix
Blend ingredients with ice
Honeydew slice garnish

MARGARITA, ANITA FAKE
House specialty glass, ice
Rim glass with salt
Pour ingredients into iced mixing glass
1 oz. non-alcoholic triple sec
2 dashes bitters
1/2 oz. Rose's Lime Juice
1 oz. cranberry juice
5 oz. Mr & Mrs T Sweet & Sour Mix
Shake and strain
Lime wedge garnish

MARGARITA, CHASTE CHILÉ
Bucket glass, ice
Rim glass with salt
Pour ingredients into iced mixing glass
1 1/4 oz. orange juice
1 oz. fresh lime juice
1-2 dashes TABASCO® Pepper Sauce
1-2 dashes jalapeño pepper juice
5 oz. sweet 'n' sour
Shake and strain
Lime wedge and jalapeño garnish

MARGARITA, FAUX MAMA

House specialty glass, ice
Rim glass with sugar
Pour ingredients into iced mixing glass
1 oz. Coco López Cream of Coconut
1/2 oz. non-alcoholic triple sec
1/2 oz. fresh lime juice
2 oz. pineapple juice
3 oz. sweet 'n' sour
Shake and strain
Pineapple wedge and cherry garnish

MARGARITA, MORAL MANGO

House specialty glass, chilled
Rim glass with Franco's Lime Green
   Citrus Margarita Salt
Pour ingredients into blender
2 oz. Frusia Mango Smoothie Base
3 oz. Dr. Swami & Bone Daddy's
   Margarita Mix
3 oz. prepared lemonade
Blend ingredients with ice
Lime wheel garnish

MARGARITA, PRISTINE PEACH

House specialty glass, chilled
Rim glass with Franco's
   Peach-Flavored Sugar
Pour ingredients into blender
2 oz. peach puree
2 oz. True Crystals Tart Lime Mix
2 oz. orange juice
2 oz. sweet 'n' sour
Blend ingredients with ice
Orange wheel garnish

MARGARITA, QUIET KISS

Bucket glass, ice
Rim glass with sugar
*Pour ingredients into
   iced mixing glass*
2 oz. cranberry juice
1/2 oz. fresh lime juice
2 oz. orange juice
2 oz. sweet 'n' sour
Shake and strain
Lime wheel garnish

TRUE CRYSTALS® MARGARITA MIXER

The margarita is the country's most frequently requested cocktail and True Crystals® has designed a line of drink mixers to build the ultimate alcohol-free margarita, regardless of the particular taste profile one's looking to recreate.

The ensemble begins with TRUE CRYSTALS® MARGARITA MIXER, a blend of fresh lime and orange juices. The juices are freeze-dried using patented technology to capture the pure, natural flavor of the fruit. With the addition of water, the enhanced granules reconstitute to their natural state. Preparation takes all of a minute.

The True Crystals® Margarita Mixer has a light, yellow-green hue and the aroma of homemade lemonade. The light-bodied mixer sports a crisp palate of fresh, tangy lime with hints of orange on the finish, ideal for building an alcohol-free margarita. It is sufficiently tart such that it will retain its zesty character even with the addition of other ingredients, or when blended with ice.

The mixer offers first class convenience and a made-from-scratch taste. It is packaged in convenient pouches for an extended shelf life.

Those who prefer to build their margaritas from the ground up should test drive the True Crystals® Sweet & Sour Mixer. Made with freeze-dried lemon juice, it is brimming with natural citrus vitality. Add in a hefty splash of True Crystals® Tart Lime Mixer. Its lively, freshly squeezed lime flavor and aroma provide the finishing touch to a great alcohol-free margarita.

MR & MRS T® STRAWBERRY DAIQUIRI-MARGARITA MIX

Mr & Mrs T is one of the most well-established and trusted names in mixology. For decades, it was the only line of drink mixes found behind great American bars. Like any great marriage, the famed couple has looked at ways to remain fresh, and over time, small changes have been made to keep the mixes at the forefront of contemporary trends.

An excellent case in point, MR & MRS T STRAWBERRY DAIQUIRI-MARGARITA MIX is light bodied, smooth and expertly balanced between sweet and tart. It has a vivid red color, a subtle bouquet and is brimming with the luscious flavor of vine-ripened strawberries. The lingering finish is flavorful, slightly tart and devoid of any cloying sweetness.

The mix is tailor-made for creating alcohol-free specialties. As the name implies, it's most often used in boosting the flavor of daiquiris and margaritas, but why stop there? For about a nickel per serving, the savory flavor of strawberries can be added to a bevy of concoctions, including piña coladas, ice cream drinks, milkshakes and smoothies.

Another great Mr & Mrs T product is Sweet & Sour Mix, a classically structured sweetened lemon juice. Sweeteners are added to throttle back some of the exuberant lemon palate, resulting in a delectably flavorful and zesty mix. Its naturally tart character provides an excellent base for scores of alcohol-free drinks, or for any concoction needing a flavorful lemon base.

Mr & Mrs T also makes a superb Piña Colada Mix that's respectfully thick, rich and tropically delicious.

MARGARITA, VIRGIN BLOODY

House specialty glass, ice
Rim glass with Franco's Lime Green
 Citrus Margarita Salt
Pour ingredients into iced mixing glass
1 oz. orange juice
1/2 oz. Rose's Lime Juice
1/4 oz. jalapeño juice
1-2 dashes TABASCO® Pepper Sauce
2 oz. Freshies Habanero Hot
 Bloody Mary Mix
2 oz. Freshies Fresh Lime Margarita Mix
Shake and strain
Lime wedge garnish

MARGARITA, VIRTUOUS PINK

House specialty glass, ice
Rim glass with pink-colored salt
Pour ingredients into iced mixing glass
1 oz. lemon syrup
3/4 oz. orange juice
1/2 oz. fresh lime juice
1 oz. cranberry juice
4 oz. Margaritaville Margarita Mix
Shake and strain
Lime wedge garnish

MARGARITA, WHOLESOME GRANNY APPLE

House specialty glass, chilled
Rim glass with Franco's Lime
 Green Citrus Margarita Salt
Pour ingredients into blender
1 oz. Torani Apple Syrup
1/2 oz. Rose's Lime Juice
4 oz. sweet 'n' sour
1-2 scoops lemon sorbet
Blend ingredients with ice
Lime wheel garnish

MERRY FRAMBOISE

Champagne glass, ice
Build in glass
Near fill with Martinelli's
 Sparkling Apple Cider
Float 1 oz. raspberry syrup
Raspberry garnish

PIÑA COLADA, BEACHY MAMA

House specialty glass, chilled
Pour ingredients into blender
3 oz. Major Peters' Piña Colada Mix
1 oz. Torani Butter Rum Syrup
2 oz. papaya juice
2 oz. sweet 'n' sour
Blend ingredients with ice
Splash club soda
Pineapple wedge and cherry garnish

PIÑA COLADA, COOLOTA

House specialty glass, chilled
Rim glass with sugar
Pour ingredients into blender
2 oz. Frusia Piña Colada Smoothie Base
1 1/2 oz. chocolate syrup
2 oz. pineapple juice
3 oz. sweet 'n' sour
2-3 scoops vanilla ice cream
Blend ingredients
Pineapple wedge garnish

PIÑA COLADA, HOLY CACTUS

House specialty glass, chilled
Pour ingredients into blender
2 oz. prickly pear puree
4 oz. pineapple juice
1 oz. orange juice
2 oz. Coco López Cream of Coconut
Blend ingredients with ice
Pineapple wedge and cherry garnish

PIÑA COLADA, IMMACULATE CHOCOLATE

House specialty glass, chilled
Pour ingredients into blender
2 oz. Torani Chocolate Mocha Sauce
2 oz. Coco López Cream of Coconut
2-3 scoops vanilla ice cream
4 oz. pineapple juice
Blend ingredients
Pineapple wedge and cherry garnish

PIÑA COLADA, KIDDIE KOALA

House specialty glass, chilled
Pour ingredients into blender
1 oz. Torani Butter Rum Syrup
1 oz. orange juice
1 oz. pineapple juice
1 oz. coconut syrup
4 oz. True Crystals Kiwi Daiquiri Mix
Blend ingredients with ice
Pineapple wedge and cherry garnish

PIÑA COLADA, MAKE-BELIEVE MANGO

House specialty glass, chilled
Pour ingredients into blender
2 oz. mango puree
1 oz. banana syrup
1 oz. Coco López Cream of Coconut
4 oz. pineapple juice
1/2 oz. half & half cream (optional)
Blend ingredients with ice
Pineapple wedge and cherry garnish

PIÑA COLADA, MOCKIN' TOASTED ALMOND

House specialty glass, chilled
Pour ingredients into blender
1 oz. coffee syrup
1 oz. orgeat (almond) syrup
1/2 oz. half & half cream (optional)
2 oz. Coco López Cream of Coconut
4 oz. pineapple juice
Blend ingredients with ice
Pineapple wedge and cherry garnish

PIÑA COLADA, PURE COFFEE

House specialty glass, chilled
Pour ingredients into blender
2 oz. cold, brewed coffee
1/2 oz. half & half cream
5 oz. Mr & Mrs T
    Piña Colada Cocktail Mix
2-3 scoops vanilla ice cream
Blend ingredients
Whipped cream and drizzle coffee
    syrup with pineapple wedge
    and cherry garnish

PIÑA COLADA, VIRGIN

House specialty glass, chilled
Pour ingredients into blender
1/2 oz. half & half cream (optional)
3 oz. Coco López Cream of Coconut
4 oz. pineapple juice
Blend ingredients with ice
Pineapple wedge and cherry garnish

PRISTINELY PEACHIE HURRICANE

House specialty glass, chilled
Pour ingredients into blender
2 oz. peach puree
1/2 oz. grenadine
1/2 oz. ReaLime Lime Juice
2 oz. pineapple juice
2 oz. orange juice
1 oz. sweet 'n' sour
Blend ingredients with ice
Orange wheel garnish

RED VELVET SPARKLER

House specialty glass, ice
Build in glass
4 oz. cranberry juice
2 oz. Torani Pink Grapefruit Syrup
Fill with club soda
Orange wheel and cherry garnish

SANGRIA PUNCH, BERRY NEW

Pitcher (64 oz.), 1/4 fill with ice
Build in pitcher
16 oz. white grape juice
3 oz. peach syrup
16 oz. cran-raspberry juice
3 oz. Frusia Raspberry Smoothie Base
3 oz. Frusia Strawberry Smoothie Base
2 oz. grapefruit juice
2 oz. orange juice
2 oz. sweet 'n' sour
Stir thoroughly
Refrigerate for 2-3 hours
Serve over ice
Lime, lemon and orange wheel garnish
Makes 8-12 servings

SANGRIA, SPARKLING NEW

House specialty glass, ice
Pour ingredients into iced mixing glass
2 oz. white grape juice
1/2 oz. peach syrup
1/2 oz. cranberry juice
1/2 oz. grenadine
1/2 oz. Rose's Lime Juice
1/2 oz. orange juice
1/2 oz. sweet 'n' sour
Shake and strain
Fill with Martinelli's
    Sparkling Apple Cider
Lime, lemon and orange wheel garnish

SANGRIA, VIRGIN

Wine glass or goblet, ice
Build in glass
3 oz. True Crystals Sangria Mix
1 oz. peach syrup
3/4 oz. grenadine
1 oz. orange juice
1 oz. sweet 'n' sour
1 oz. ReaLime Lime Juice
Lime, lemon and orange wheel garnish

TORANI-POLITAN

House specialty glass, ice
Pour ingredients into iced mixing glass
3/4 oz. Torani Raspberry Syrup
1/4 oz. Rose's Lime Juice
6 oz. prepared lemonade
Shake and strain
Lemon twist garnish

TRANQUIL SUNSET

House specialty glass, ice
Pour ingredients into iced mixing glass
1 oz. Torani Mandarin Orange Syrup
5 oz. sweet 'n' sour
Shake and strain
Fill with ginger ale
Float 1 oz. Torani Pomegranate Syrup
Orange wheel garnish

Chapter 2

Alcohol-Free Marys, Caesars and Sangritas

The Bloody Mary is perhaps the most singular drink in the lexicon of mixology. It's a drink every bartender regularly makes and yet no two bartenders make it the same. When made well, the Bloody Mary is an absolute work of art—robust, nutritious and loaded with taste.

What makes the Bloody Mary such a classic crowd-pleaser, though, has little to do with vodka. As any Bloody Mary aficionado will attest, the secret behind the drink's extraordinary popularity lies almost entirely in the mix. So cast aside any outdated notions that the Bloody Mary must necessarily be prepared with alcohol, and begin serving delicious, exuberant libations without giving the recipient the possibility of a hangover.

As a point of interest, the first Bloody Mary is credited to Fernand Petiot, a bartender at famed Harry's New York Bar in Paris in 1924. Paris at the time was a haven for Russian exiles, including members of the Smirnoff family. He dubbed his original concoction of all things the "Bucket of Blood." While the drink caught on, the name didn't, and it soon became known as the Bloody Mary, likely in honor of Mary Tudor, the unfortunate daughter of King Henry VIII.

Making a world class, alcohol-free Bloody Mary is a deceptively simple process. Most scratch recipes start with a base of tomato juice, however, a stellar mix can be made using Clamato, or V-8 juice. The next step is to add modifiers, which give the base some personality and character. Classic choices such as Worcestershire sauce, prepared horseradish and TABASCO® Pepper Sauce are typically considered a must. Optional ingredients include A-1 Sauce, Mexican hot sauce or pureed salsa, soy sauce, olive juice, cilantro, fresh lime or lemon juice, Angostura Bitters and jalapeño pepper juice.

The true creative artistry comes into play when adding seasonings. Celery salt, salt and black pepper are just the beginning. Cayenne pepper, cumin, paprika, crushed dried red peppers, onion powder, garlic salt or powder, thyme, Chinese mustard, seasoned salt, chili powder, cardamom, Italian seasoning, ginger, Old Bay Seasoning and basil round out the shopping list. And whether a pinch, a teaspoon, or a dash of any of the above is used should be a matter left entirely up to the artist's discretion.

The final touch to any noteworthy alcohol-free Bloody Mary is the garnish. More than a mere embellishment, the garnish should be considered an ingredient in the drink. The classic garnish is celery. Use only the tender, interior pieces, not the fibrous, outer stalks. Also, leave the leafy greens on; it gives the celery a fresh, attractive appearance.

A fresh lime or lemon wedge is the other standard garnish on a Bloody Mary. They add a delightful citrus tang to the drink. But no need to stop there. Optional garnishes include scallions, olives, pearl onions, cooked and peeled shrimp (or prawns), beef jerky, Slim Jims, asparagus, tomatoes and cucumber spears, pepperoncinis or small jalapeño peppers.

Creating the Ultimate Alcohol-Free Bloody Mary

Few great works of art are created on the first attempt. Sample several batches until the perfect taste profile is attained. This begs the question, is there really a definitive Bloody Mary? Because it is so subjective and dependent on personal preferences, the answer is likely no.

On the other hand, nearly all great Bloody Marys share similar attributes. For one thing, great Marys have a thick, almost chewy consistency and appear hearty enough to pass as a meal. They also must have at least some spice and a slight kick. A world class Bloody Mary needn't scald the larynx, but it does need to stimulate the senses and impress the recipient that they're still alive.

People looking for a sensational drink with no possibility of regret deserve to be treated to a spirited alcohol-free Bloody Mary. To that end, here are the secrets to the quintessential hangover-free Mary.

Tip #1: Taste Test Bloody Marys Over Ice — Taste testing is integral to the process of creating a Mary masterpiece. It is important to always sample the mix over ice, a practice that will best simulate game-like conditions. In addition to cooling the mix, the ice will naturally dilute the drink's consistency and spicy character, factors that must be taken into consideration. Anticipating the diluting effects of ice is crucial.

Tip #2: Use Caution When Playing with Fire — Some people want an alcohol-free Bloody Mary hot and spicy to the point of being nearly combustible. There are others who prefer to survive the experience fully intact. The concept of hot and spicy is a relative one, so caution needs to be exercised when adding heat, regardless of whether it's in the form of spice or sauce. It is far easier to add more heat to a Bloody Mary than to calm one down.

Tip #3: Consistency Counts — Where Mary is concerned, thin is not in. A Bloody Mary with a rich, thick consistency immediately conveys quality. It suggests that the drink is substantial, nutritious and that it was prepared with a bevy of vitamin enriched products. It is similar to stew—the thicker and heartier the soup, the more life sustaining it is.

Tip #4: First Impressions Matter — The Bloody Mary is a tall, iced drink and must therefore be served in a tall, good looking glass. The drink deserves a glass with a capacity of 12-16 ounces, anything less is an insufficient portion. In addition, present the Mary in a glass with some aesthetic appeal to it. Offering a guest a fabulous Bloody Mary in a plain, nondescript glass is like displaying a magnificent painting in a cardboard frame.

Tip #5: Garnish and Embellish — The embellishments sitting atop a Bloody Mary contribute to both the flavor of the drink and the enhancement of its overall visual appeal. It's hard to over do it when it comes to garnishes, so don't be stingy, however, do consider how much volume the garnishes will take up in the drink. It's a mistake to add so many finishing touches that the drink overflows its glass.

Tip #6: Deliver the Sizzle with an Edible Swizzle — Why has a celery stalk accompanied nearly every Bloody Mary ever served? While opinions differ, one thing is undeniably true; celery is an effective and attractive swizzle stalk. It allows the recipient to both stir the drink and have a nosh. In a democracy there is no law mandating that celery accompany the Bloody Mary. Indeed, there are several other options when it comes to edible swizzles, namely asparagus, jerky, cucumber spears or something akin to a Slim Jim. Regardless of whether it's edible or not, provide guests with an attractive means of stirring their Bloody Marys.

Tip #7: Storing Bloody Mary Mix — When storing Bloody Mary mix, affix a label to the container and write the date that the mix is prepared. This will ensure that old product past its prime is not served to guests. Most mixes have a refrigerated shelf life of a week or less; after which, they should be discarded.

Creative Alcohol-Free Mary Variations

Bloody Marys are a rare, sublime pleasure, but they do not represent the boundary of all that is possible. A few simple alterations to a recipe can transform the flavor of a Bloody Mary into something different, an entirely new taste experience for guests to revel in. So have fun, experiment and create a masterpiece.

The most famous of these thematic variations is the Bloody Caesar, a classic Mary made with a healthy dose of clam juice, or more likely, Clamato Juice. The drink is almost an institution in Canada, where its popularity far exceeds that of the conventional Bloody Mary.

Other creative options include the Bloody Cajun, which gets its personality from onion powder, thyme, red pepper and paprika, and the Italian Maria, a tempting offering made with garlic powder, paprika and prepared Italian seasonings. The Tex-Mex Mary is partially fueled by chili powder and cumin.

An additional splash or two of olive juice is all that's needed to create a Bloody Olive, while beef bouillon is the driving force behind the Virgin Bloody Bull. A Maria Mexicana is prepared with salsa, hot sauce and garnished with a small handful of tortilla chips.

Other variations to consider are the Bloody Michilata, which contains non-alcoholic beer as an ingredient, and the Mango Mary, a savory libation prepared in a blender with cubes of ripe mangoes. The Bloody Olfactory is a fiery combination of horseradish, a raw oyster and Bloody Mary mix. A slight variation on the theme is the Peppy Oyster, a Louisiana specialty made with TABASCO® Pepper Sauce, prepared horseradish, cocktail sauce, diced avocado, cilantro, jalapeño peppers, green onions and a raw oyster.

Sangrita is an alcohol-free Mexican concoction popular with tourists and natives alike. It is similar in character to a Bloody Mary, but it is built upon a base comprised of orange juice and tomato juice.

Making the Grade with Bottled Mary Mixes

If searching for the perfect scratch recipe sounds more involved than the time at-hand permits, bottled Bloody Mary mixes offer a viable, cost-effective alternative. The new generation of fresh and sassy bottled Bloody Mary mixes rival the most delectable house recipes, and the field of entrants run from hot to scalding. Invariably these products originated as specialties of the house and were thought too good to be kept secret. In nearly every case, they were right.

These Bloody Mary mixes are produced in a wide variety of styles to match nearly any needs. Most important, they are quality items loaded with great taste. Sure, the process may require sampling several different brands before making a selection, but the result may well be worth it.

There's no reason on Earth why you can't make a few additions to a bottled Bloody Mary mix to make it better. Splash in some olive juice, add a little crushed, roasted garlic or a heaping tablespoon of fresh salsa. A stitch here and a tuck there may be all that's needed to make a signature drink capable of capturing the imagination.

The reviews of several bottled Bloody Mary mixes are featured in this chapter. They are representative of exactly how far civilization has progressed.

ANGRY OYSTER

Bucket or house specialty glass, ice
Rim glass with salt
Pour ingredients into blender
1 tbs. avocado, diced
1 tbs. chives
1 tsp. cilantro, chopped
1/2 tsp. prepared horseradish
1 tbs. cocktail sauce
2-3 dashes TABASCO® Jalapeño
    Pepper Sauce
6 oz. Clamato Bloody Caesar Mix
Blend ingredients
Float raw oyster
Green onion garnish

BASIC SCRATCH
BLOODY MARY MIX

Large covered jar (64 oz.)
Pour ingredients into jar
2 oz. Worcestershire sauce
7-8 dashes TABASCO® Pepper Sauce
2-3 dashes Angostura Bitters
2 tbs. celery salt
1 tbs. black pepper
1/2 tbs. salt
46 oz. tomato juice
*Mix ingredients, taste-test over ice,
    adjust for personal taste*

BLOODY BLIZZARD

House specialty glass, ice
Rim glass with salt
Pour ingredients into blender
1/3 cup jicama, cubed
1/2 oz. fresh lemon juice
2-3 dashes pepper sauce
6 oz. Bloody Mary mix
Blend ingredients
Lime wedge garnish

BLOODY BOOST

House specialty glass, ice
Rim glass with salt
Build in glass
2 oz. orange juice
Splash grapefruit juice
Fill with TABASCO®
    Bloody Mary Mix
Orange wheel garnish

MAJOR PETERS'
BLOODY MARY MIXES

Created in the 1960s by a gentleman named Peter Majors, the popular line of Bloody Mary mixes are made from 94% California tomatoes and a flavor package that sports a minimum of 40 spices, peppers and herbs.

The brand's flagship, all-natural MAJOR PETERS' ORIGINAL BLOODY MARY MIX, is deliciously tame, with its heat generated primarily in the finish. The mix has good texture and consistency. While reserved, compared to the other Mary mixes in the family, the Original version is exceptionally adaptable, making it an ideal undercarriage for almost any creative inspiration.

Major Peters' "The Works!" Bloody Mary Mix is made with impressive portions of just about every classic ingredient. It brings a respectable amount of heat to bear on the palate and is chock full of tasty morsels of onions, peppers and horseradish. Remarkably thick, savory and wholesome, "The Works" is a masterpiece straight from the bottle.

For those Mary enthusiasts with a taste for a zesty concoction with some heat, Major Peters' Hot & Spicy Bloody Mary Mix is the one to try. It is chunky and quite substantial. While not for the weak at heart, this marvelous mix is brimming with the spicy, bold flavors of fresh horseradish, chiles, onions and garlic.

Major Peters' Salsa Bloody Mary Mix has an authentic salsa flavor. It is skillfully balanced and loaded with the garden fresh flavors of chiles, garlic, peppers and sweet tomatoes. Its heat builds in intensity, gradually diminishing into a long, flavorful finish.

TABASCO® EXTRA SPICY BLOODY MARY MIX

When it comes to alcohol-free Bloody Marys—some people want a nearly combustible drink loaded with pepper and fiery spice, while others prefer their cocktails flavorful, yet somewhat restrained. TABASCO® brand, the most famous name in heat since 1868, offers two prepared mixes to satisfy the entire Mary consuming universe. They are exuberant, masterfully spiced and nearly impossible to resist.

One of the gems produced by McIlhenny Company of Avery Island, Louisiana, is TABASCO® EXTRA SPICY BLOODY MARY MIX, an aromatic, richly textured and flavorful premium mix. It features the delicious heat of famed TABASCO® Pepper Sauce with a blend of tomato juice, Lea & Perrins Worcestershire Sauce, lime and lemon juice, horseradish and a bevy of spices and herbs for a marvelously robust taste. McIlhenny Company adds a higher concentration of their pepper sauce to create this mix, which is immediately evident. The mix finishes beautifully with lingering heat and moderately hot pepper flavor.

The company also makes a tamer version dubbed TABASCO® Bloody Mary Mix. The flavor includes TABASCO® Pepper Sauce, but the heat factor is scaled back. It's a thoroughly enjoyable base for an alcohol-free specialty.

McIlhenny Company has cultivated distinctively flavored *Capsicum frutescens* peppers and turned them into world renowned TABASCO® brand Pepper Sauce. Likely Louisiana's most famous product, TABASCO® Pepper Sauce is made using red peppers aged in oak barrels, local Avery Island salt and distilled white vinegar.

BLOODY MARTIN
House specialty glass, ice
Rim glass with salt
Build in glass
4 oz. non-alcoholic beer
Fill with Mr & Mrs T Bloody Mary Mix
Lime wedge garnish

BLOODY OLIVE
Bucket glass, ice
Rim glass with salt
Build in glass
1/2 oz. olive juice
Fill with Bloody Mary mix
Olive and celery garnish

BLOODY OLFACTORY
Bucket or house specialty glass, ice
Rim glass with salt
Build in glass
1/2 tbs. prepared horseradish
Near fill with Bloody Mary mix
Float raw oyster
Lemon wedge and celery garnish

CALIFORNIA DREAMIN' MARY
Bucket glass, ice
Rim glass with salt
Pour ingredients into blender
1/4 cucumber, diced
1/4 avocado, diced
1 small tomato, diced
6 oz. Bloody Mary mix
Blend ingredients
Cherry tomato and
avocado slice garnish

CRUSHED CLAM
Bucket glass, ice
Rim glass with salt
Pour ingredients into blender
1 small tomato, diced
1-2 dashes pepper sauce
2 pinches crushed red pepper
2 pinches crushed black pepper
2 pinches crushed thyme leaves
2 pinches crushed basil
8 oz. Clamato Tomato Cocktail
Blend ingredients
Celery garnish

DRINK YOUR VEGGIES, MARY

House specialty glass, ice
Rim glass with salt
Pour ingredients into blender
1 small tomato, diced
1 radish
1 pickle spear
1/4 red pepper
1/4 green pepper
3-4 dashes hot sauce
1/2 tsp. prepared horseradish
1/2 tsp. Worcestershire sauce
2 pinches black pepper
6 oz. V-8 juice
Blend ingredients
Celery garnish

FIERY FEAST

House specialty glass, ice
Rim glass with salt
Build in glass
2 tbs. cucumber, finely diced
1/2 tsp. prepared horseradish
1/2 oz. fresh lemon juice
4-5 dashes TABASCO® Pepper Sauce
1-2 pinches black pepper
Fill with TABASCO® Extra Spicy
   Bloody Mary Mix
Cucumber spear garnish
Note: For variety, replace cucumber
   with other vegetables

FIVE-ALARM MARY

House specialty glass, ice
Rim glass with salt
Build in glass
1 pinch crushed red pepper
2 pinches chili powder
3 pinches black pepper
4 dashes pepper sauce
5 dashes jalapeño
   pepper sauce
1/2 oz. fresh lemon juice
1/2 fill Freshies Habanero
   Hot Bloody Mary Mix
1/2 fill Freshies Original
   Bloody Mary Mix
Lemon wedge and
   celery garnish

MR & MRS T®
BLOODY MARY MIX

Mr & Mrs T is the first name in Bloody Mary mix, and despite their longevity, they have continually tinkered with their mixes to ensure that they are perfectly in step with the times. A few sips will confirm that they've more than accomplished their objectives for a great mix.

Like most highly successful Mary mixes, this venerable, thoroughly enjoyable brand is prepared according to a closely held, proprietary recipe and contains a lengthy list of fresh herbs, peppers and spices. The original Mr & Mrs T is a classically structured Bloody Mary mix. It has an easy to drink, silky smooth consistency and a fresh, lightly seasoned, tomato-y palate. The flavorful finish is marked with notes of celery and onion.

Mr & Mrs T is an ideal drink base to feature at a Bloody Mary bar, primarily because of its understated character and enormous creative potential.

Following the consumer trend toward thicker, heartier mixes, Mott's introduced MR & MRS T RICH & SPICY BLOODY MARY MIX. Its recipe is loaded with spice and vitality, The mix has just enough heat to wake the taste buds, but not enough to overwhelm the palate, which is a difficult line to walk. The Rich & Spicy Bloody Mary has a hefty body, smooth consistency and the zesty flavors of fresh horseradish and green peppers. The enduring finish is laced with the prominent flavor of jalapeño peppers and a moderate amount of spicy heat.

CLAMATO®
TOMATO COCKTAIL

Created in Alberta, Canada in 1969, Clamato is a singular cocktail mix that has attained a broad, international following, especially in Canada where it is revered as something of a national treasure. While best known as the heart and soul of the Bloody Caesar, MOTT'S CLAMATO TOMATO COCKTAIL and its siblings are frequently being served as entities in their own right.

Clamato is smooth, light and fabulously refreshing. It has a subtle onion and garlic bouquet, a slightly sweet tomato flavor and is completely devoid of any heat. The fresh taste of clam juice is understated and most noticeable on the clean, crisp finish. Embellishing the mix with a lime or lemon wedge garnish greatly enhances its seafood character.

Those looking for a bit more excitement out of life should sample Clamato Bloody Caesar Cocktail Mix. The light-bodied mix has a savory bouquet of onion, garlic and a hint of celery, and a palate ideally balanced between sweet tomatoes and spicy garlic. The moderate amount of heat doesn't overstay its welcome, while the hearty flavor of clam juice shows itself on the finish. The mix makes a sensational, hangover-free Bloody Caesar directly from the bottle.

Also from Mott's is Clamato Picante, a smooth bodied, easy to drink mix. It has a peppery bouquet and a jalapeño-laced palate with moderate, lingering heat. The finish is an enviable marriage of pepper, tomato and clam juice. Its consistency and bold character are guaranteed to satisfy the most particular Bloody Caesar aficionado.

FREE-TOE MARY
House specialty glass, ice
Rim glass with salt
Pour ingredients into blender
6-8 Fritos
2 oz. spicy corn relish
2-3 dashes hot sauce
2 pinches ground cumin
6 oz. Bloody Mary mix
Blend ingredients
Lemon wedge and fritos garnish

FRENCH MARY
House specialty glass, ice
Rim glass with salt
Build in glass
1/2 tbs. Dijon mustard
1/4 tsp. celery seed
2-3 pinches salt
2-3 pinches black pepper
Fill with Bloody Mary mix
Asparagus garnish

GARLIC CHARM
House specialty glass, ice
Rim glass with salt
Build in glass
1/2 tsp. crushed garlic
1/2 tsp. prepared horseradish
2-3 pinches lemon pepper
2-3 pinches oregano
Fill with Freshies Smooth 'n' Mild
Bloody Mary Mix
Lemon wedge garnish

GIVE ME A
STEAK, MARY
Bucket glass, ice
Rim glass with salt
Build in glass
3/4 oz. steak sauce
2 pinches black pepper
Fill with Bloody Mary mix
Red and green
pepper garnish

ITALIAN VIRGIN MARIA

Bucket glass, ice
Rim glass with salt
Build in glass
1/8 tsp. Italian seasoning
2 pinches garlic powder
2 pinches paprika
2 pinches celery salt
Fill with Bloody Mary mix
Lime wedge and celery garnish

MARIA MEXICANA

Bucket glass, ice
Rim glass with salt
Pour ingredients into blender
1 scallion, chopped
1 white onion ring, chopped
1/2 tsp. fresh cilantro, chopped
2-3 dashes Mexican hot sauce
Fill with Major Peters'
    Salsa Bloody Mary Mix
Scallion and tortilla chips garnish

NIPPON MARI

Bucket glass, ice
Rim glass with salt
Build in glass
1/4 tsp. soy sauce
1/4 tsp. balsamic vinegar
1/4 tsp. sesame seeds
1/4 tsp. wasabi
1 tsp. sugar
Fill with Bloody Mary mix
Cucumber wheel garnish

NO BLAME, NO SHAME

House specialty glass, ice
Rim glass with salt
Pour ingredients into blender
2-3 water chestnuts
1/2 oz. fresh lemon juice
2 pinches oregano
2 pinches garlic salt
6 oz. Mr & Mrs T
    Bloody Mary Mix
Blend ingredients
Lemon wedge and
    parsley garnish

FRESHIES HABANERO HOT BLOODY MARY MIX

Born and raised in Telluride, Colorado, Freshies is a small company whose name accurately conveys their basic approach to creating products. The entire range of Freshies all natural Bloody Mary mixes is crafted entirely from garden fresh ingredients and without artificial preservatives.

Those who want a Bloody Mary mix to cause sweat to pour from their brows should test-drive FRESHIES HABANERO HOT BLOODY MARY MIX, a flavorful mix with near fission capability. This dynamic little number is made with Worcestershire sauce, fresh onions, horseradish, garlic, dill, lemon juice, black pepper, hot sauce and tangy Dijon mustard. Its considerable heat is derived from a healthy dose of habanero chiles. This Freshies mix has as much life as any that has ever graced a glass.

The company's Original Bloody Mary Mix tastes like it took hours of careful preparation, instead of coming straight from a bottle. It has an intriguing, complex palate that creates a lot of activity in the mouth. The mix is thick, expertly seasoned and loaded with bits of chewy vegetables. Freshies Original has respectable heat that lingers throughout the long, slightly smoky finish.

Freshies also makes a Smooth 'N' Mild Bloody Mary Mix. It too has good body, great seasonings and a well-balanced flavor. The mix is relatively mild, although that somewhat stretches the definition. This enticing Bloody Mary mix also sports a roasted, smoky finish, one reminiscent of a well-made barbecue sauce. It's excellent on its own, or as the base of an alcohol-free specialty.

PROUD MARY

Bucket glass, ice
Rim glass with salt
Pour ingredients into blender
1/4 orange, peeled
1/2 oz. fresh lemon juice
2 pinches paprika
2 pinches ginger powder
6 oz. Bloody Mary mix
Blend ingredients
Lemon wedge garnish

PURE MANGO MARY

Bucket glass, ice
Rim glass with salt
Pour ingredients into blender
1/2 cup mango, cubed
1/2 tsp. prepared horseradish
1-2 dashes TABASCO® Pepper Sauce
1/8 tsp. chili powder
1/8 tsp. ginger powder
2 pinches black pepper
6 oz. Bloody Mary mix
Blend ingredients
Lemon wedge and mango garnish

SINLESS CAJUN MARY

Bucket glass, ice
Rim glass with salt
Build in glass
1/4 tsp. onion powder
1/8 tsp. crushed thyme leaves
1 pinch crushed red pepper
2 pinches paprika
Fill with Major Peters'
    "The Works" Bloody Mary Mix
Lime wedge and celery garnish

SMOKY MARY

Bucket glass, ice
Rim glass with salt
Build in glass
1 tbs. hickory barbecue sauce
1-2 dashes Worcestershire sauce
1-2 dashes soy sauce
2 pinches black pepper
Fill with Bloody Mary mix
Lime wedge and celery garnish

SWEDISH MARY

Bucket glass, ice
Rim glass with salt
Build in glass
1/8 tsp. caraway seed
1-2 pinches ground fennel
1-2 pinches salt
1-2 pinches black pepper
Fill with Bloody Mary mix
Lime wedge and celery garnish

TEXAS MARY

Bucket or house specialty glass, ice
Rim glass with salt
Build in glass
1/8 tsp. chili powder
2 pinches ground cumin
1 oz. chunky salsa
Fill with Bloody Mary mix
Lime wedge and celery garnish

VIRGIN BLOODY BULL

Bucket glass, ice
Rim glass with salt
Build in glass
1/2 fill beef broth
1/2 fill Bloody Mary mix
Lime wedge and celery garnish

VIRGIN BLOODY CAESAR

House specialty glass, ice
Rim glass with salt
Build in glass
1 1/2 oz. clam juice
Fill with Bloody Mary mix
Lime wedge and celery garnish

WASABI MARY

Bucket glass, ice
Rim glass with salt
Build in glass
1/2 tbs. grated carrot, chopped
1/4 tsp. soy sauce
1/8 tsp. ginger powder
1/8 tsp. wasabi paste
1/4 tsp. crushed red pepper
Fill with Major Peters' Original
    Bloody Mary Mix
Lemon wedge and celery garnish

Chapter 3

Ice Cream Drinks Appeal to the Kid in All of Us

Sometimes determining what people *really* want to drink takes imagination and creative thinking. Guests often don't even know what they want, and ironically, it's rarely limited to what they *say* they want. But rest assured, people want to drink something that'll make their day or perfect their evening.

There is a lesson to be learned from those who work in the great restaurants of the world. Even in this day and age of health-awareness and fitness videos, chefs still take great pains to prepare trays full of tempting desserts and profit handsomely as a result. Few people go out to dinner with the intent to calorie-bulk on a dessert. Yet, when faced with a tray of devilishly irresistible treats, their heads slowly nod yes and they make a selection.

Unfortunately, many behind the bar have lost touch with this time-tested marketing concept. Tempting guests with irresistible, dessert-like libations is a "can't miss" proposition. It appeals to the child within all of us, and whether they admit it or not, people are attracted most to the instant gratification of taste.

Ice cream or frozen yogurt is a nearly perfect medium for liqueurs, cordials, and distilled spirits. Its sweet, creamy consistency accepts a wide variety of flavors, making it extremely easy to be creative. Ice cream and frozen yogurt enjoy a nearly universal appeal, an observation validated by a trip down almost any major thoroughfare counting the number of ice cream parlors and frozen yogurt stores.

Creating Ice Cream Classics

Here's an easy to conduct experiment to prove that an alcohol-free drink can be every bit as gratifying as a dessert on a plate.

Start by placing two heaping scoops of French vanilla ice cream in a blender. Add a ripe banana, 1/2 cup of fresh raspberries, an ounce of chocolate syrup, a splash of whole milk and blend thoroughly. Pour the contents into a chilled house specialty glass and garnish with a dollop of whipped cream and a drizzle of chocolate syrup. While there is no such thing as a universal crowd-pleaser, this concoction comes awfully close.

When preparing blended ice cream drinks, there are only two basic tips to keep in mind regarding technique. If after blending the ingredients the resulting drink is too thick to pour easily, add more milk and blend again. Conversely, if the resulting drink is too thin and more closely resembles flavored milk, drop in another scoop or two of ice cream and reblend.

Vanilla ice cream is most frequently used in specialty drinks, likely because it provides an almost neutral base upon which to add a wide array of flavors. There is, however, no reason to create exclusively with vanilla ice cream. There are at least 31 flavors from which to choose, so experiment. In addition to ice cream, there's also frozen yogurt, sherbet and sorbet. Each will lend a different taste and texture to the concoction.

There are now several products that look and taste like ice cream, but don't need to be stored in a freezer. True Crystals Crème Mixer, Island Oasis Vanilla Ice Cream and Maui Ice Cream Mix are designed for commercial use and are excellent substitutes for ice cream. They're easy to use and deliver a lot of ice cream flavor for pennies per ounce.

Ice cream specialty drinks are typically flavored with different types of modifiers, one being fresh fruit, such as bananas, strawberries, raspberries, melon and peaches. Other flavorings include chocolate, caramel, butterscotch syrup, peanut butter, fruit juice, iced coffee or espresso, crushed cookies and candy bars. Modifiers come in many different forms, so don't get fenced in.

Torani syrups and sauces are also invaluable to the process of creating world class ice cream libations. The Italian-born, alcohol-free syrups are slightly sweetened and available in a huge variety of flavors for home or commercial use. Their syrups run the gamut from raspberry, watermelon and Tiramisu to Almond Roca®, macadamia and chocolate biscotti, while their sauces include chocolate mocha, white chocolate mocha and caramel. The creative possibilities of blending ice cream and Torani syrups and sauces are unlimited.

Creating these alcohol-free signature drinks is hardly arduous. Consider pairing chocolate ice cream and Mandarin oranges with espresso coffee, or strawberry ice cream with Torani Amaretto Syrup. Then again, who said anything about being limited to using ice cream? Imagine combining fresh kiwis with lime sherbet, or papayas with lemon sorbet.

Another delectable option is a swirl, which is made by serving two different ice cream concoctions "swirled" together in the same glass. Choose two drinks with complementary flavors but distinctly different looks. They taste as intriguing as they appear.

On the extreme end of the creativity curve is the Mel's Chocolate/PB/Nana Shake, a delicious creation made with chocolate syrup, peanut butter, milk, vanilla ice cream, and a fresh banana. It's so big and satisfying that it could be served as an entrée. Equally sensational is the Raspberry Banana Split, a swirled specialty consisting of three separate layers. The bottom is made with Torani Coffee Syrup and chocolate ice cream, the second is banana syrup and vanilla ice cream, and the top layer is raspberry syrup and French vanilla.

In many respects, this is about exceeding expectations and indulging guests' desires. Thoroughly decadent and loaded with pleasure, ice cream libations are guaranteed to do just that.

ALMOND MOCHA ROCA MILKSHAKE

House specialty glass, chilled
Pour ingredients into blender
2 oz. Torani Almond Roca® Syrup
4 oz. cold, brewed coffee
3-4 scoops chocolate ice cream
Blend ingredients
Whipped cream garnish

APPLE BETTY'S SHAKE

House specialty glass, chilled
Rim glass with cinnamon sugar
Pour ingredients into blender
1/2 cup apple sauce
2 oz. milk
1 tbs. honey
1/2 tsp. cinnamon
1/8 tsp. nutmeg
1/2 graham cracker
3-4 scoops vanilla ice cream
Blend ingredients
Whipped cream and drizzle
   caramel sauce garnish

BANANAS FOSTER SHAKE

House specialty glass, chilled
Pour ingredients into blender
1 banana, peeled
1 oz. Torani Butter Rum Syrup
1 oz. Torani English Toffee Syrup
4 oz. milk
3-4 scoops vanilla ice cream
Blend ingredients
Whipped cream and dust
   with ground cinnamon garnish

BLUE-RASPBERRY GUILT-FREE DELITE

House specialty glass, chilled
Pour ingredients into blender
1 oz. blueberry syrup
1 oz. raspberry syrup
4 oz. fat-free milk
3-4 scoops vanilla
   frozen yogurt
Blend ingredients with ice
Whipped cream and
   crushed almonds garnish

TORANI CHOCOLATE MOCHA FLAVORING SAUCE

Something magical happens when the devilishly rich topping of chocolate sauce or caramel meets waiting ice cream. Flavors meld together, consistencies begin to change and a swirling look appears. Naturally, the better the sauce, the more magical the process.

There is perhaps no sauce more skillfully crafted or brimming with flavor than those produced by R. Torre & Company of San Francisco, makers of the delectable TORANI CHOCOLATE MOCHA FLAVORING SAUCE. This premium sauce is made with an impressive line-up of chocolate flavorings, including famed Dutch cocoa, Dutch breakfast cocoa and cocoa butter, and sweetened with pure cane sugar. The result is an absolutely luxurious sauce capable of adding a tremendous burst of flavor to any concoction, ice cream based or not.

R. Torre & Company also makes two other sensational sauces. Torani White Chocolate Flavored Mocha Sauce is made from cocoa butter, sweetened condensed skim milk, natural flavors and pure cane sugar. For lovers of white chocolate, this is the real deal. It is velvety smooth and loaded with the singular aroma and taste of white chocolate.

The other is Torani Caramel Sauce, which contains butter, heavy cream and natural flavorings. It, too, is a sumptuous delight. Caramel sauce is the essential ingredient in caramellas, a savory caffe-mocha-style drink.

All three sauces enjoy scores of applications, including ice cream drinks, shakes, hot cocoas, soda drinks and a wide assortment of coffee concoctions.

TRUE CRYSTALS®
VANILLA CRÈME MIXER

Making ice cream drinks at home is no more complicated than getting the necessary ingredients out of the freezer, revving up the blender, then sitting back and enjoying the fruits of one's labor. The process is slightly more involved, however, when making these specialty drinks at a restaurant or bar. Keeping a commercial bar stocked with ice cream can result in a soggy, melted mess. With no freezer capacity behind the bar, ice cream drinks are a hit-or-miss proposition.

That was before True Crystals® solved the problem with the introduction of VANILLA CRÈME MIXER, an innovative dairy product designed for use in specialty ice cream drinks. The mixer is made using patented technology from sweetened, freeze-dried condensed skim milk. The resulting enhanced granules reconstitute to their original state with the addition of water. Preparation takes all of a minute or two.

True Crystals® Vanilla Crème Mixer has the look, taste and aroma of home-made ice cream. The mixer has a wafting vanilla bouquet and an exceptionally thick and rich consistency, one similar in texture to melted ice cream. The palate is slightly sweet and adapts easily to any flavor added to it. For a change of pace try their Orange Crème Mixer. Same ease of use as the Vanilla Crème Mixer with a delicious orange flavor.

These mixers have taken all of the hassle out of making ice cream specialty drinks. Each package of mixer yields the equivalent of a quart of ice cream, but unlike ice cream, it need only be refrigerated to stay fresh. Essentially, True Crystals® has gone ice cream one better.

BOO-BERRY VANILLA FREEZE
House specialty glass, chilled
Pour ingredients into blender
1 oz. blueberry syrup
6 oz. True Crystals Vanilla Crème Mix
1/2 cup mixed frozen berries
Blend ingredients with ice
Whipped cream garnish

BROWN VELVET MILKSHAKE
House specialty glass, chilled
Pour ingredients into blender
2 oz. Torani Root Beer (Classic) Syrup
4 oz. milk
3-4 scoops vanilla ice cream
Blend ingredients
Whipped cream garnish

CHERRY GARCIA SHAKE
House specialty glass, chilled
Pour ingredients into blender
1 oz. cherry syrup
2 oz. cherry pie filling
4 oz. milk
3-4 scoops vanilla ice cream
Blend ingredients
Add 1/2 Hershey's Chocolate Bar
*Note: Flash blend until chocolate
    bar breaks into small pieces*
Whipped cream and drizzle chocolate
    syrup garnish

CHOCOLATE COVERED
PEAR SHAKE
House specialty glass, chilled
Pour ingredients into blender
1 1/2 oz. Torani
    Pear Syrup
1 oz. Torani Chocolate
    Mocha Sauce
4 oz. milk
3-4 scoops vanilla
    ice cream
Blend ingredients
Whipped cream
and drizzle chocolate
syrup garnish

CHOCOLATE RASPBERRY DELICIOUS SHAKE
House specialty glass, chilled
Pour ingredients into blender
2 oz. raspberry puree
1 oz. chocolate syrup
4 oz. milk
3-4 scoops vanilla ice cream
Blend ingredients
Whipped cream garnish

CLASSIC CHOCOLATE MOCHA MILKSHAKE
House specialty glass, chilled
Pour ingredients into blender
2 oz. Torani Chocolate Mocha Sauce
4 oz. milk
3-4 scoops vanilla ice cream
Blend ingredients
Whipped cream garnish

FOOLED-FRESH MANGO SHAKE
House specialty glass, chilled
Pour ingredients into blender
2 oz. mango puree
4 oz. milk
3-4 scoops vanilla ice cream
Blend ingredients
Whipped cream garnish

FOOLED-FRESH PEACH FREEZE
House specialty glass, chilled
Pour ingredients into blender
2 oz. peach puree
4 oz. milk
3-4 scoops vanilla frozen yogurt
Blend ingredients with ice
Whipped cream garnish

FOOLED-FRESH RASPBERRY FREEZE
House specialty glass, chilled
Pour ingredients into blender
2 oz. raspberry puree
4 oz. milk
3-4 scoops vanilla frozen yogurt
Blend ingredients with ice
Whipped cream garnish

FOOLED-FRESH STRAWBERRY SHAKE
House specialty glass, chilled
Pour ingredients into blender
2 oz. strawberry puree
4 oz. milk
3-4 scoops vanilla ice cream
Blend ingredients
Whipped cream garnish

4TH OF JULY TROPICAL FREEZE
House specialty glass, chilled
Pour ingredients into blender
1/2 cup watermelon, cubed
2 oz. pineapple juice
2 oz. Mauna La'i Island Guava Juice
3-4 scoops pineapple sorbet
Blend ingredients with ice
Pineapple wedge, blueberries and
    American flag garnish

JAMOCA COCASHAKE
House specialty glass, chilled
Pour ingredients into blender
3 oz. cold, brewed coffee
3 oz. milk
2 oz. chocolate syrup
3-4 scoops vanilla ice cream
Blend ingredients
Whipped cream and drizzle
    coffee syrup garnish

MUDDY SLIDE SHAKE
House specialty glass, chilled
Pour ingredients into blender
1 oz. Torani Irish Cream Syrup
1 oz. Torani Coffee Syrup
4 oz. milk
3-4 scoops vanilla ice cream
Blend ingredients
Whipped cream and drizzle
    chocolate syrup garnish

ORANGE DREAMSICLE SHAKE

House specialty glass, chilled
Pour ingredients into blender
3 oz. orange juice
1 oz. vanilla syrup
2-3 scoops vanilla ice cream
2-3 scoops orange sorbet
Blend ingredients
Whipped cream garnish

PEANUT BUSTER SWIRL

House specialty glass, chilled
Pour ingredients into blender
1/4 cup peanuts, salted
4 oz. milk
3-4 scoops vanilla ice cream
Blend ingredients
2 oz. hot fudge
*Pour blended ingredients and hot fudge
into serving glass, swirling fudge
throughout mixture.*
Whipped cream and
crushed peanuts garnish

PETER PIPER
PUMPKIN SHAKER

House specialty glass, chilled
Pour ingredients into blender
1 oz. Torani Ginger Spice Syrup
2 oz. prepared pumpkin puree
4 oz. milk
3-4 scoops vanilla ice cream
Blend ingredients
Whipped cream and dust
with ground cinnamon garnish

PIÑA COOLATA MILK SHAKE

House specialty glass, chilled
Pour ingredients into blender
2 oz. Dole Pineapple Juice
1 oz. Coco López Cream of Coconut
1/4 cup Dole Pineapple Chunks
2 oz. milk
3-4 scoops vanilla ice cream
Blend ingredients
Whipped cream and
pineapple wedge garnish

RUBY TOPAZ SWIRL

House specialty glass, chilled
Object is to create a swirled drink
Step 1: Pour ingredients into blender #1
2 oz. Frusia Raspberry Smoothie Base
2 oz. milk
1-2 scoops vanilla ice cream
Blend ingredients
Step 2: Pour ingredients into blender #2
2 oz. Frusia Peach Smoothie Base
2 oz. milk
1-2 scoops vanilla ice cream
Blend ingredients
*Pour each blended concoction into serving
glass, allowing the mixes to swirl.*
Whipped cream garnish

STRAWBERRY
ALMOND MILKSHAKE

House specialty glass, chilled
Pour ingredients into blender
2 oz. Torani Almond Roca® Syrup
4 oz. milk
3-4 scoops strawberry ice cream
Blend ingredients
Whipped cream and
crushed almonds garnish

THIN MINT COOKIE SHAKE

House specialty glass, chilled
Pour ingredients into blender
3-4 chocolate mint cookies
1 oz. chocolate syrup
4 oz. milk
3-4 scoops vanilla ice cream
Blend ingredients
Whipped cream garnish

VANILLA COFFEE SHAKE

House specialty glass, chilled
Pour ingredients into blender
1 oz. coffee syrup
1 oz. vanilla syrup
4 oz. milk
3-4 scoops vanilla ice cream
Blend ingredients
Whipped cream garnish

Chapter 4

Smoothies Break into the Popular Mainstream

Some of us still subscribe to the theory that anything high in nutritional value must taste awful. Likewise, if something tastes bad, it must be just what the doctor ordered. It is, however, difficult to cling to this point of view after taking a long draw from a smoothie. Even its name sounds comforting.

In fact, smoothies could possibly be the best of all things. They're delicious and nutritious, which for many, is a completely alien concept. Nevertheless, smoothies are healthy, potable meals with the look, feel and taste of fruit milkshakes. In this time-conscious, nutrient-depleted day and age, smoothies are something of a panacea, a 21st century concoction perfectly in step with the times.

So what is a smoothie? Essentially, they are blended drinks made with fruit, non-fat frozen yogurt, sherbet and/or sorbet and ice. Some are even dairy-free. But there's no reason to stop there.

For example, mega-popular Jamba Juice, a national chain of smoothie purveyors, adds such highly beneficial things as vitamins, minerals, fiber, herbs, amino acids, soy protein and phytonutrients to their various blended concoctions. They have smoothies designed to do everything from provide a boost of energy or fight a cold, to bolster one's immunity or to help shed a few unwanted pounds. All this and they're sumptuous too.

Creating Smoothie Classics

The essential first step in preparing a classic smoothie drink is to plug in the blender, after that, let the creative juices flow. To give the process a shove in the right direction, think of smoothies as containing four basic elements, namely juice(s), fruits, modifiers and base mix.

Juice — If it's true that an apple a day keeps the doctor away, smoothies could seriously dent the medical profession. In addition to the likes of orange, apple, pineapple and cranberry juice, consider adding other less conventional juices such as carrot, grape, raspberry, peach nectar, apple cider, tangerine, beet, kiwi, passion fruit nectar, strawberry nectar and mango, to name but a few.

It is a continuing mystery of nature exactly how and why various juices taste great blended together. Unexplained as it may be, feel free to mix and match various juices according to personal taste and preference. No need to justify inspiration.

Fruits & Vegetables — In addition to adding flavor and nutrients to a smoothie, blending in fruit boosts the drink's fiber content and enhances its texture and consistency. Since these are blended drinks, for the best consistency freeze fruit prior to use.

Featuring frozen strawberries, bananas, apples, or raspberries in a smoothie are an excellent beginning. But it's a big world and fruit comes in all shapes and sizes. Smoothies should reflect this diversity. To that end, some of the possible fruit selections to be mixed and matched include frozen or fresh peaches, cantaloupe, honeydew, apricots, pears, watermelon, oranges, tangerines, pineapples, carrots, beets, dates, avocados, papaya, persimmons, pitted cherries, mangos, blackberries and blueberries.

Modifier — Much of the fun begins with the addition of modifiers, those things that give the creation its individuality. Modifiers come in two basic categories. There are those ingredients intended to improve the quality of the recipient's life. Perhaps they're antioxidants, such as vitamins A, E and beta-carotene, or fiber, such as wheat germ and oat bran, or sources of protein, such as bee pollen, brewers yeast and soy. Also falling into this health store variety of modifiers are flaxseed oil, ginko biloba, ginseng, lecithin, protein powders, wheat grass, echinacea, calcium, folic acid and vitamins B, C and D.

Then there are smoothie modifiers that just plain taste great. They may be intended to add flavor or provide a welcome touch of sweetness. Either way, these are ingredients that are bound to satisfy the kid in all of us. This tasty category includes, but is not limited to chocolate or caramel sauce, coffee, agave nectar, espresso coffee, Reese's peanut butter cups, candy bars, walnuts, vanilla extract, cinnamon, nutmeg, grenadine, chai tea, coconut cream, coconut milk, peanut butter, raspberry or strawberry preserves, honey, malted milk powder, maple syrup, cookies, (dried) unsweetened coconut and brown sugar.

Base — The final consideration is the foundation of the drink. Because of its low-fat nature, frozen yogurt is a popular choice as a smoothie base. It has a rich, creamy texture and comes in a slew of interesting flavors. Others may prefer using soy milk or soy yogurt for health reasons.

Both sorbet and sherbet are frequently featured in smoothies. They are easy to use and also available in a wide variety of flavors. Finally, people looking for nothing but pleasure tend to prefer building their smoothies on a base of ice cream.

Fortunately, there are a number of superior smoothie mixes available on the market. Offering a delicious, convenient and cost-effective method of preparing smoothies. These mixes can be paired with fruit, or used as a fabulous base upon which to create a smoothie masterpiece.

So rev up the blender and join one of the hottest and most delectable beverage trends in the country.

SMOOTHIES — Any smoothie can be customized with one or more nutritious additives. Always check with a physician before making changes to your diet.

BLUE ALOHA SMOOTHIE
House specialty glass, chilled
Pour ingredients into blender
1/2 cup blueberries
6 oz. pineapple juice
3-4 scoops vanilla frozen yogurt
Blend ingredients with ice
Pineapple wedge garnish

CARIBBEAN DREAM SMOOTHIE
House specialty glass, chilled
Pour ingredients into blender
1/2 cup mango, fresh or frozen
1/2 cup peaches, fresh or frozen
1-2 scoops orange sorbet
1-2 scoops lemon sorbet
Blend ingredients with ice
Orange wheel garnish

CARROT APPLE SMOOTHIE
House specialty glass, chilled
Pour ingredients into blender
4 oz. carrot juice
4 oz. unfiltered apple juice
4 oz. Island Oasis Frozen Non-Fat Yogurt Mix
Blend ingredients with ice

CHOCOLATE BANANA SMOOTHIE
House specialty glass, chilled
Pour ingredients into blender
1 banana, peeled
2 oz. chocolate syrup
4 oz. milk
3-4 scoops vanilla frozen yogurt
Blend ingredients with ice
Banana slice garnish

CRYSTALS INTERNATIONAL FOODS™ VANILLA SMOOTHIE BASE

Smoothies have become standard fare in coffee shops and cafes around the country. They are popularly sold everywhere from shopping malls and bowling centers to tourist attractions and sporting venues. The smoothie boom has created the need for CRYSTALS INTERNATIONAL FOODS™ VANILLA SMOOTHIE BASE, a product so delicious and easy-to-use that anyone with some ice and a blender can be in the smoothie business.

This innovative product is made using patented technology. The base is portioned in pouches and comprised of tiny granules that reconstitute with the addition of water. Although the base remains fresh in the refrigerator for weeks, it will be used long before that.

The Vanilla Smoothie Base provides a blank canvas upon which great things are possible. The base has a thick, creamy body and a vanilla hue. It is subtly aromatic with enticing wafts of vanilla and tastes slightly sweet. The most invaluable characteristic of this smoothie base is its universal mixability. It is primed and ready to accept any flavor or health-conscious array of ingredients capable of fitting into a blender.

Its ease-of-use and agreeable personality make the base an ideal product for use in creating smoothie specialties. With it a classic smoothie is only a few moments away. For example, add some sliced strawberries, fresh raspberries, a splash of True Crystals® Kiwi Daiquiri Mixer, grape juice and the Vanilla Smoothie Base then blend with ice. *Voila.*

Crystals International Foods™
A DIVISION OF CRYSTALS INTERNATIONAL INC.

Vanilla Smoothie Base

Made with Crystals™ Freeze-dried Powders

Net Wt. 21.3 oz.
(604.0 Grams)

Makes 1
U.S. Quart

ISLAND OASIS BANANA FROZEN BEVERAGE MIX

As a company, Island Oasis is dedicated to the art and science of making frozen drinks. They produce a highly successful line of drink mixes, as well as patented equipment designed to make the process of making a wide variety of frozen concoctions problem-free and virtually foolproof, smoothies included.

Illustrative of the company's level of creativity and expertise is the ISLAND OASIS BANANA FROZEN BEVERAGE MIX. It is a creamy, flavorful product tailor-made for use behind the bar. Sold frozen in quart containers, the pourable mix has a refrigerated shelf life of three weeks after opening.

It's well known that mushy, overripe bananas make the most flavorful drinks and that keeping shriveled black fruit behind the bar is more hassle than it's worth. Now there's an alternative. Island Oasis has captured the luscious aroma and flavor of overripe bananas in their frozen puree. The mix is thick, richly textured and delicious.

In addition to their classic banana mix, the Island Oasis line of all-natural flavors includes peach, guava, passionfruit, mango, raspberry and strawberry. The mixes contain no additives, preservatives, artificial flavorings, or colors.

The line of frozen drink mixes also includes Island Oasis Cappuccino, a sweetened blend of milk and 100% Colombian coffee concentrate. In the hands of a skilled mixologist, it is a creative bonanza. Both the Island Oasis Frozen Nonfat Yogurt Mix and their Vanilla Ice Cream Mix make splendid bases for smoothies. The vanilla flavored mixes are like blank canvases. Add the desired flavors and blend away.

CRANBERRY CRAZED SMOOTHIE
House specialty glass, chilled
Pour ingredients into blender
3 oz. cranberry juice
1/4 cup strawberries, fresh or frozen
1/4 cup blueberries, fresh or frozen
4 oz. plain yogurt
2-3 scoops raspberry sherbet
Blend ingredients with ice
Strawberry garnish

CRANBERRY ORANGE SMOOTHIE
House specialty glass, chilled
Pour ingredients into blender
1/2 cup blueberries, fresh or frozen
2 oz. cranberry juice
2 oz. orange juice
4 oz. Crystals International Foods
    Vanilla Smoothie Base
Blend ingredients with ice
Orange wheel garnish

CUCUMBER BLISS SMOOTHIE
House specialty glass, chilled
Pour ingredients into blender
2-3 mint leaves
    1/4 cucumber, peeled
    3 oz. apple juice
    1-2 scoops lemon
        frozen yogurt
    1-2 scoops lemon sorbet
    Blend ingredients with ice
    Lemon wheel garnish

GUAVA JUBILEE
House specialty glass, chilled
Pour ingredients into blender
3 oz. Kern's Guava Nectar
1/4 cup mango,
    fresh or frozen
2 oz. prepared limeade
3-4 scoops vanilla
    frozen yogurt
Blend ingredients with ice
Lime wheel garnish

HAWAII-YOU-TO-DAY?

House specialty glass, chilled
Pour ingredients into blender
1/2 cup tropical fruit salad
2 oz. orange juice
4 oz. Maui Smoothie Starter
Blend ingredients with ice
Orange wheel garnish

IN THE MOO'D

House specialty glass, chilled
Pour ingredients into blender
1/2 banana, peeled
4 oz. milk
2 oz. chocolate syrup
2 oz. peanut butter
3-4 scoops vanilla frozen yogurt
Blend ingredients with ice
Banana slice garnish

KEY LIME CRANBERRY BREEZE SMOOTHIE

House specialty glass, chilled
Pour ingredients into blender
1 oz. Rose's Lime Juice
1 oz. ReaLime Lime Juice
3 oz. cranberry juice
2 oz. Frusia Raspberry
   Smoothie Base
4 oz. plain yogurt
Blend ingredients with ice
Lime wheel garnish

KIWI-BERRY BOOSTER SMOOTHIE

House specialty glass, chilled
Pour ingredients into blender
1/2 cup kiwi, peeled
   and sliced
1/4 cup strawberries,
   fresh or frozen
4 oz. orange juice
3-4 scoops vanilla
   frozen yogurt
Blend ingredients with ice
Strawberry garnish

TORANI FRUSIA MANGO SMOOTHIE BASE

Sometimes a blast of the exotic is just what the doctor ordered to break up the week. By definition, exotic means something that's strange and unusual. Well, unless someone happens to live in the tropics, mangos qualify as exotic, and there is no better source for this delectable fruit than TORANI FRUSIA MANGO SMOOTHIE BASE.

Torani Frusia is a line of sumptuous whole fruit purees suited for fruit smoothies. It has a compelling, true-to-fruit bouquet and a genuinely singular texture, similar to fruit preserves or marmalade. The mix has the look of pureed mangos and the added pectin gives it a marmalade-like consistency. The flavor is a straightforward proposition of savory ripe mangos.

The mixes come in cost-effective, 64-ounce tubs designed to accommodate a pre-proportioned pump, which makes it possible to quickly dispense the product in measured doses. Each is shelf-stable but refrigerating overnight once opened extends the shelf-life.

Produced by R. Torre & Company of San Francisco, this premium mix is made using fresh fruit, pure cane sugar and natural flavorings. A proprietary blending process results in an amazingly rich and thick puree. In addition to mango, the Frusia line also includes strawberry, raspberry, peach, mixed berry, kiwi fruit and piña colada.

While Torani Frusia was created for use in smoothies, there are scores of applications for it behind the bar. It can be used to add flavor to a wide range of beverages including lemonade, ice cream, juices, teas and cocktails.

MAUI SMOOTHIE STARTER

There are times that we all need a little help getting started. Knowing this, the good folks at Maui Beverages have concocted a marvelous mix to use as a neutral base for making smoothies. Appropriately named MAUI SMOOTHIE STARTER, it is a pasteurized, all natural product made from vanilla and non-fat liquid yogurt, without the tart yogurty taste.

As a refrigerated product, it is far more convenient to use behind the bar or coffee shop than grocery store yogurt. Simply pour the mix into an iced blender, flavor at will and blend. There's no scooping or soggy container to contend with. Maui Smoothie Starter has a velvety smooth consistency and a delicious vanilla flavor.

Maui Beverages also produces a line of delectable fruit mixes designed for smoothies and other specialty frozen drinks and cocktails. They are masterfully prepared purees of fresh fruit, lemon juice and sweeteners. The purees have the look, smell and taste of real fruit. They are richly textured and bursting with vivid, sweet and tart flavors.

The Maui mixes are available in strawberry, raspberry, mango, banana, peach, lemon ice, margarita and piña colada. The fruit-based products have a shelf life of 2 years when frozen. Once thawed, they keep their freshness for upwards of 2 months and are stored in the refrigerator.

The Maui Frozen Cappuccino Mix has the marvelous flavor and aroma of fresh brewed coffee with just a touch of sweetness. It makes an excellent base for scores of frozen specialty drinks, including frozen cappuccinos, mochaccinos and cappuccino mudslides.

KIWI-LIME SUNRISE SMOOTHIE

House specialty glass, chilled
Pour ingredients into blender
3/4 cup kiwi, peeled and sliced
1 oz. ReaLime Lime Juice
4 oz. prepared limeade
2-3 scoops lemon sherbet
Blend ingredients with ice
Lemon wheel garnish

MAID IN A MINUTE ORANGE SMOOTHIE

House specialty glass, chilled
Pour ingredients into blender
2 oz. orange juice
2 tbs. honey
4 oz. Maui Peach Fruit Blend Mix
4 oz. vanilla yogurt
Blend ingredients with ice
Orange wheel garnish

MANGO-A-GO-GO SMOOTHIE

House specialty glass, chilled
Pour ingredients into blender
2 oz. Frusia Mango Smoothie Base
3 oz. orange juice
2-3 scoops pineapple sherbet
Blend ingredients with ice
Pineapple wedge garnish

MEL-BAN-STRAW-BEE SMOOTHIE

House specialty glass, chilled
Pour ingredients into blender
1/2 cup melon, cubed
1/2 cup strawberries, fresh or frozen
1 banana, peeled
4 oz. apple juice
3-4 scoops vanilla frozen yogurt
Blend ingredients with ice
Strawberry garnish

MELON MARVEL
   SMOOTHIE
House specialty glass, chilled
Pour ingredients into blender
1/2 cup watermelon, cubed
1/2 cup honeydew melon, cubed
1 oz. ReaLime Lime Juice
1 tbs. honey
4 oz. orange juice
4 oz. vanilla yogurt
Blend ingredients with ice
Watermelon cube garnish

MOCHA DIVINITY
   SMOOTHIE
House specialty glass, chilled
Pour ingredients into blender
2 oz. chocolate syrup
1 oz. coffee syrup
4 oz. milk
3-4 scoops vanilla frozen yogurt
Blend ingredients with ice

NECTAR OF AMBROSIA
   SMOOTHIE
House specialty glass, chilled
Pour ingredients into blender
1 oz. pineapple juice
2 oz. apple juice
1 oz. orange juice
1 oz. Coco López Cream of Coconut
1 banana, peeled
3 oz. Crystals International Foods
   Vanilla Smoothie Base
Blend ingredients with ice
Orange wheel garnish

PAPAYA PINEAPPLE
   PASSION FRUIT SMOOTHIE
House specialty glass, chilled
Pour ingredients into blender
1/2 cup papaya, cubed
1/2 cup pineapple, crushed
4 oz. Mauna La'i Paradise Passion Juice
3-4 scoops vanilla frozen yogurt
Blend ingredients with ice
Pineapple wedge garnish

PEACHY MORNING
   SMOOTHIE
House specialty glass, chilled
Pour ingredients into blender
1/2 cup peaches, fresh or frozen
1/2 cup papaya, fresh or frozen
4 oz. orange juice
3-4 scoops vanilla frozen yogurt
Blend ingredients with ice
Orange wheel garnish

PICK ME UP
   CITRUS FREEZE
House specialty glass, chilled
Pour ingredients into blender
1 cup Dole Pineapple Chunks
1 oz. ReaLemon Lemon Juice
4 oz. orange juice
1 tbs. honey
Blend ingredients with ice
Fill with club soda
Lemon wheel garnish

PIÑABERRY SMOOTHIE
House specialty glass, chilled
Pour ingredients into blender
1/2 banana, peeled
1/2 cup berries, fresh or frozen
6 oz. pineapple juice
3-4 scoops vanilla frozen yogurt
Blend ingredients with ice
Pineapple wedge garnish

PINK PARADISE FREEZE
House specialty glass, chilled
Pour ingredients into blender
4 oz. Island Oasis Banana Frozen
   Beverage Mix
1/2 cup mangos, cubed
1/2 cup strawberries, frozen
3 oz. cranberry juice
3-4 scoops vanilla frozen yogurt
Blend ingredients with ice
Strawberry garnish

POWER PLUS SMOOTHIE

House specialty glass, chilled
Pour ingredients into blender
1 banana, peeled
1/4 cup trail mix with dates
2 oz. carob powder
4 oz. apple juice
3-4 scoops vanilla frozen yogurt
Blend ingredients with ice
Dust carob powder

PURE PUMPKIN SMOOTHIE

House specialty glass, chilled
Pour ingredients into blender
1/4 cup prepared pumpkin puree
1/2 banana, peeled
1/4 tsp. cinnamon
1/8 tsp. nutmeg
1/8 tsp. ginger
1 tbs. honey
4 oz. apple juice
3-4 scoops vanilla frozen yogurt
Blend ingredients with ice
Dust ground cinnamon

SPICED PEACH
FREEZE SMOOTHIE

House specialty glass, chilled
Pour ingredients into blender
1/2 cup peaches, fresh or frozen
4 oz. lemon-flavored club soda
1/8 tsp. ground ginger
1 tsp. honey
6 oz. lemon yogurt
Blend ingredients with ice
Peach slice garnish

STRAWBERRY
SUNRISE SMOOTHIE

House specialty glass, chilled
Pour ingredients into blender
1 banana, peeled
1/2 cup strawberries, fresh or frozen
5 oz. apple juice
3-4 scoops vanilla frozen yogurt
Blend ingredients with ice
Strawberry and banana slice garnish

TIME FOR A RUN
BREAKFAST SMOOTHIE

House specialty glass, chilled
Pour ingredients into blender
1/2 cup blueberries, fresh or frozen
4 oz. blueberry yogurt
1 tbs. honey
1 tbs. dry milk powder
8 oz. skim milk
Blend ingredients with ice
Orange wheel garnish

TROPICAL COCONUT
SMOOTHIE

House specialty glass, chilled
Pour ingredients into blender
2 oz. orange juice
2 oz. pineapple juice
2 oz. Coco López Cream of Coconut
1/2 banana, peeled
3-4 scoops vanilla frozen yogurt
Blend ingredients with ice
Orange wheel garnish

VERY BERRY APRICOT
DELITE SMOOTHIE

House specialty glass, chilled
Pour ingredients into blender
1/2 cup berries, fresh or frozen
2 oz. apricot nectar
4 oz. apple juice
3-4 scoops vanilla frozen yogurt
Blend ingredients with ice
Berry garnish

ZESTY CANTALOUPE
SMOOTHIE

House specialty glass, chilled
Pour ingredients into blender
1/2 cup cantaloupe, cubed
1/4 cup raspberries, fresh or frozen
1/4 cup blackberries, fresh or frozen
4 oz. apple juice
1 oz. fresh lemon juice
1/4 tsp. lemon peel, finely grated
4 oz. lemon yogurt
Blend ingredients with ice
Cantaloupe cube garnish

Chapter 5

Kids' Drinks! Making the Grade with Minor Leaguers

A s almost any parent will attest, kid's menus are a lifesaver. They're loaded with items created specifically with young folk in mind. These menus empower kids and give them an opportunity to order food they like and in portions that they can easily handle.

Open up the typical kid's menu and what likely won't be within its pages are specialty drinks marketed exclusively to kids. If there are special food items for kids, why not offer them special drink choices as well? Why make them suffer with the usual selections of post-mix sodas and orange juice?

Well, the fact of the matter is that good things happen when an eating establishment looks to enhance the dining experience for kids by offering them special things to drink. Showing consideration for kids generates loyalty in their parents, as well as increases the odds that the whole family will want to return another night.

If generating good will isn't motivation enough, there's also the little matter of generating more profits. While most of these small-fry specialties retail for less than their adult counterparts, they deliver relatively the same amount of gross profit. All things considered, marketing signature drinks to the minor leaguers makes good sense.

Creating Classics for Kids

"Special" to kids usually means being served a great looking, great tasting concoction, served in a sensational looking glass that mom and dad wouldn't normally let them drink from at home. The realm of possibilities has expanded greatly since the days of the kiddie cocktails and Shirley Temples. The philosophical orientation is to create specialty drinks that will knock their socks off.

For example, consider the Mel's Chocolate/PB/Nana Shake. Start with a tall specialty glass with a 16- to 20-ounce capacity. Paint the inside of the glass with ribbons of chocolate syrup. Place 3-4 scoops of vanilla ice cream, 4 ounces whole milk, a large, ripe banana, 2 ounces chocolate syrup and 2 tablespoons of creamy peanut butter into the blender. Thoroughly blend, pour into the painted specialty glass and garnish with whipped cream.

So where to start? Here are some ideas that should help you create an Olympic class beverage program for our country's youth.

Lemonade — This great American beverage is a good starting point. Using Torani syrups you can feature an unlimited variety of flavorful, colorful combinations, such as blueberry lemonade or strawberry lemonade. Two other creative options are to blend lemonade with sorbet and fresh fruit into a slushy drink, or mix Hawaiian Punch with lemonade and ice for a novel specialty.

Smoothies — Kids love smoothies, as long as they don't know that they're drinking something borderline healthy. Smoothies need not be more complicated than blending juice, fruit, yogurt and ice together. For fun, blend in a few cookies as well.

The Spin Doctor of Drinks — Frozen drinks are tall, colorful, delicious and extremely lucrative. There are scores of creative blended specialty drinks ideally suited for young people. For instance, starting with an alcohol-free strawberry daiquiri or piña colada, add a banana, some vanilla ice cream, a few sweet strawberries and a healthy dash of chocolate syrup. The creation will be something they'll talk about in school.

Consider promoting a swirled blended drink for kids. Swirls are made by combining in the same glass, two blended drinks with different looks but complementary flavors. An excellent example is swirling together an alcohol-free raspberry daiquiri and vanilla milkshake in the same glass.

Soda Drinks — Looking at life from a kid's perspective, every restaurant that their parents take them to offers the same selection of sodas. Why not offer these future voters sodas with unusual flavors that aren't typically stocked like black cherry, root beer, vanilla, or kiwi strawberry? These sodas can also be used to create fabulous floats, such as Mandarin lime soda and lemon sorbet, vanilla soda and chocolate ice cream, or cream soda and Cherry Garcia ice cream. Add a splash of a complementary Torani syrup flavor to push the drink into the exceptionally tasty range.

Don't overlook the enduring popularity of the root beer float and the Coke ice cream float. Also, Martinelli Sparkling Cider is a kid favorite. Serve it by the glass or use it as the base of a signature drink.

Hot Cocoa and Chocolate Milk — When in doubt, call on a kid's best friend, chocolate. Make hot cocoa something truly special by floating a scoop of ice cream on top with whipped cream and a sprinkle of shaved chocolate. Hot cocoa can also be served with a layer of frothed chocolate milk on top. Chocolate milk can be served as a tall, slushy specialty drink by flash blending with ice in a blender.

The Power of Presentation — Sure these drinks need to taste great, but they also have to look spectacular. Market kid's drinks in tall, durable specialty glasses. Frozen blueberries or grenadine are great sources for color, and a few dashes of vanilla extract creates an irresistible aroma. The *coup de grace* is using a red licorice stick with its ends cut off instead of a straw.

Have fun and think like a kid. The drinks will be a smash hit with the kids and their parents, too.

KIDS DRINKS — Though these are all technically drinks, feel free to use a spoon whenever the urge hits you. Some of these delicious specialties are stand-up-to-a-straw thick!

APOLLO BLAST OFF

House specialty glass, chilled
Pour ingredients into blender
8 oz. Hawaiian Punch
3-4 scoops orange sherbet
Blend ingredients with ice
Pop rocks (when served) garnish

CHERRY CHOCOLATE SODA

House specialty glass, chilled
Build in glass
2/3 fill seltzer
2 oz. maraschino cherry juice
1-2 scoops chocolate ice cream
Whipped cream and drizzle
  cherry juice garnish

CHOCOLATE CHIMP

House specialty glass, chilled
Pour ingredients into blender
1/2 banana, peeled
2 oz. chocolate syrup
6 oz. milk
3-4 scoops vanilla ice cream
Blend ingredients
Barrel of Monkeys toy garnish

COLAR POLAR BEAR CHILL

House specialty
  glass, chilled
*Pour ingredients
  into blender*
8 oz. cola
3-4 scoops vanilla ice cream
Blend ingredients
Marshmallow and mini
  marshmallows garnish

YOO-HOO® CHOCOLATE DRINK

Natale Olivieri was the owner of a small, New Jersey company that bottled carbonated, fresh fruit drinks. One day in the early 1920s, Olivieri was helping his wife preserve tomatoes when it occurred to him that the same heating method might be effective at preserving a chocolate drink he had been working on. After lengthy experimentation, he eliminated the spoilage problem and created an all natural beverage, one without chemicals or preservatives. Olivieri named it YOO-HOO CHOCOLATE DRINK and began selling it to a chocolate-starved nation.

Yoo-hoo Chocolate Drink has not changed since its debut eight decades ago. It is made from non-fat milk, whey, cocoa, sweeteners and natural flavoring. The non-carbonated drink is 99% fat- and caffeine-free, and because of its dairy content, should be refrigerated after opening. For those who need a little variety in life, Yoo-hoo is available in three additional styles: Chocolate-Banana Yoo-hoo, Strawberry Yoo-hoo and Yoo-hoo Lite, a low-cal version of the original.

Yoo-hoo well deserves its status as a timeless American classic. The experience of drinking a Yoo-hoo begins with the mind-captivating aroma of cocoa. It immediately fills the mouth with the determined flavor of dairy fresh milk chocolate, only its body is somewhat lighter and silkier than chocolate milk.

Yoo-hoo Chocolate Drink can be served as the base of an ice cream float, or make a Yoo-hoo soda by adding a dose of seltzer and two scoops of ice cream. Its most dramatic role is as the headline performer in a milkshake. The drink is also a natural paired with iced coffee.

FRUIT JUICY RED HAWAIIAN PUNCH®

In 1934, three California men began developing a tropical tasting syrup to add to their company's line of ice cream toppings. After three years of laboring in a converted garage, the trio introduced a fruit punch concentrate called Leo's Hawaiian Punch. Soon afterwards, their customers reported that the syrup was far better mixed in water as a drink than as an ice cream topping. During the war, the company began selling the punch as a drink concentrate and renamed it Hawaiian Punch.

The now famous recipe includes pineapple, apple, pear, passion fruit and orange juices, as well as papaya and guava purees.

FRUIT JUICY RED HAWAIIAN PUNCH is one of the most successful and recognizable brand names in the country. It has a classic punch taste—full, varied and loaded with tropical nuances. Its semi-sweet start quickly yields the floor to the tart, fruit-laced finish. The drink is vitamin C enriched to 100% R.D.A.

The Hawaiian Punch line has grown over the years, and now includes five variations on the original theme, including Strawberry Surfin', Green Berry Rush, Orange Ocean, Grape Geyser and pineapple driven Tropical Punch.

This famous beverage enjoys numerous applications behind the bar in alcohol-free specialty drinks. It is excellent when blended with lime or lemon sorbet, or any number of flavored sherbets. The Hawaiian Punch concentrate is also a marvelous way to flavor a specialty milkshake.

FROBSCOTTLE
House specialty glass, chilled
Pour ingredients into blender
1/4 cup kiwi, peeled and sliced
1/4 cup raspberries, fresh or frozen
1/2 oz. ReaLime Lime Juice
1 oz. plain yogurt
6 oz. prepared lemonade
Blend ingredients with ice
Fill with cream soda
Cherry garnish

HAWAIIAN FRUIT FREEZE
House specialty glass, chilled
Pour ingredients into blender
8 oz. Hawaiian Punch
1/4 cup strawberries, fresh or frozen
1/4 cup pineapple chunks
Blend ingredients with ice
Orange wheel, cherry and pineapple
    wedge garnish

HERMIONE'S MAGIC POTION
House specialty glass, ice
Build in glass
Near fill Martinelli's
    Sparkling Apple-Grape Cider
Pop rocks (when served) garnish

HOWDJA-LIKE-
A-LITTLE-PUNCH?
House specialty glass
Build in glass
1/2 fill ice
    Fill remainder of glass
        with cherries, orange
        and lemon wheels
1/2 fill Squirt
1/2 fill Hawaiian Punch
Red licorice straw
    (snip ends) garnish

HOWDY, PARDNER!
House specialty glass, ice
Build in glass
Near fill with grape soda
Float 1/2 oz. Rose's
    Lime Juice
Lime wheel and
    cherry garnish

KID'S COSMIC COOLER

House specialty glass, chilled
Pour ingredients into blender
3 oz. cranberry juice
3 oz. apple juice
1 oz. Rose's Lime Juice
Splash grenadine
Blend ingredients with ice
Fun straw, cherry and lime wheel garnish

MAUNA KAPOWNI KAZAAM

House specialty glass, crushed ice
Build in glass
2/3 fill Mauna La'i ¡Mango Mango! Juice
1/3 fill lemon-lime soda
Orange wheel and cherry garnish

MEL'S KID'S CHOCO BUTTERSCOTCH SHAKE

House specialty glass, chilled
Pour ingredients into blender
1 oz. butterscotch sauce
1 oz. chocolate syrup
4 oz. milk
3-4 scoops vanilla ice cream
Blend ingredients
Whipped cream and drizzle
   butterscotch sauce garnish

MEL'S KID'S CHOCO/PB/NANA SHAKE

House specialty glass, chilled
Pour ingredients into blender
2 oz. chocolate syrup
1 banana, peeled
2 tbs. peanut butter
4 oz. milk
3-4 scoops vanilla ice cream
Blend ingredients
Whipped cream and sprinkle
   shaved chocolate garnish

P.B. & J.

House specialty glass, chilled
Pour ingredients into blender
2 oz. strawberry puree
3 tbs. peanut butter
6 oz. grape juice
2-3 scoops vanilla ice cream
Blend ingredients

PURPLE PEOPLE EATER

House specialty glass, chilled
Pour ingredients into blender
1/4 cup blueberries, fresh or frozen
1 oz. Rose's Lime Juice
4 oz. prepared lemonade
3-4 scoops raspberry sherbet
Blend ingredients
Fun straw and maraschino cherry garnish

RAINBOW COLADA

House specialty glass, chilled
Pour ingredients into blender
4 oz. pineapple juice
2 oz. Coco López Cream of Coconut
2 tbs. colored sprinkles
3-4 scoops vanilla ice cream
Blend ingredients
Whipped cream, colored sprinkles and
   maraschino cherry garnish

RASMANIAN DEVIL

House specialty glass, chilled
Pour ingredients into blender
4 oz. raspberry puree
1/2 banana, peeled
6 oz. apple juice
Blend ingredients with ice

RASPBERRY CIDER FREEZE

House specialty glass, chilled
Pour ingredients into blender
8 oz. Martinelli's Sparkling Cider
3-4 scoops raspberry sorbet
Blend ingredients with ice
Drizzle raspberry syrup

SHREK'S SMOOTHIE SNACK

House specialty glass, chilled
Pour ingredients into blender
1/4 cup kiwi, peeled and sliced
1/4 cup peaches, fresh or frozen
6 oz. apple juice
2-3 scoops lime sherbet
Blend ingredients
Gummie worms garnish
   (push 3-4 partially into drink)

SIMPLY FRUITALICIOUS

House specialty glass, chilled
Pour ingredients into blender
1/4 cup fruit, fresh or frozen
1 oz. blueberry syrup
4 oz. milk
Blend ingredients with ice
Orange wheel and strawberry garnish

SMURF SWEAT

House specialty glass, ice
Build in glass
1/2 fill Squirt
1/2 fill prepared lemonade
Drizzle blueberry syrup
Orange wheel and cherry garnish

STRAWBERRY
MANGO CHILLER

House specialty glass, chilled
Pour ingredients into blender
1/2 cup strawberries, fresh or frozen
1/4 cup mango chunks, fresh or frozen
6 oz. cranberry juice
2-3 scoops orange sherbet
Blend ingredients with ice
Strawberry garnish

STRAWBERRY SMASH

House specialty glass, ice
Build in glass
2 oz. strawberry puree
1 oz. Rose's Lime Juice
Fill with lemon-lime soda
Strawberry garnish

SPARKLING BLOSSOM

House specialty glass
Build in glass
1 strawberry dropped into
   bottom of glass
Fill with ice
1/3 fill Martinelli's Sparkling Cider
1/3 fill prepared lemonade
1/3 fill white grape juice
Drizzle grenadine
Lemon wheel and strawberry garnish

TRIPLE DECKER
CARAMEL DELITE

House specialty glass, chilled
1/2 oz. caramel sauce
   drizzled in bottom of glass
Pour ingredients into blender
1/4 cup Milk Duds candy
4 oz. milk
3-4 scoops vanilla ice cream
Blend ingredients
2 oz. caramel sauce
*Pour blended concoction into serving
   glass, swirling the caramel sauce*
Whipped cream and drizzle
   caramel sauce garnish

WORMS AND DIRT

House specialty glass, chilled
Pour ingredients into blender
6 oz. apple juice
3 Oreo cookies
3-4 scoops vanilla ice cream
Blend ingredients
Gummie Worms and
   Raisinets garnish
   (Submerge 3-4 worms
   partially into drink)

YOO-HOOZE-MOOZ-JUIZE

House specialty glass, chilled
Pour ingredients into blender
4 oz. Yoo-hoo
4 oz. cola
3-4 scoops vanilla ice cream
Blend ingredients
Whipped cream and drizzle
   chocolate syrup garnish

Chapter 6

Specialty Products and the Sizzle They Add to Drinks

There are certain universal truths. For instance, we could all use a break in our week. Mondays are challenging for everyone and workdays seem much longer than 9 hours. So, when a guest orders something alcohol-free, why not give them a drink with some pizzazz, something that raises an eyebrow and elicits an appreciative smile. After all, if it doesn't have sizzle, why serve it?

Such is the working philosophy behind detailing a drink. The concept is twofold. First, it's often the finishing touch on a drink that casts the first impression. Second, adding that one extra something to a recipe is all that's needed to transform an ordinary drink into an extraordinary one. The process is like detailing a car; brilliance comes from paying attention to the small stuff. This chapter is devoted to the special items that exist only to advance the cause of detailing a drink.

Products with Appeal

Fun and light-hearted enjoyment can be found almost everywhere. Even something as commonplace as a plastic sword pick can spark a swashbuckling duel at a bar. It's just the thing for helping a CEO-type to get in touch with his inner child. A cool swizzle stick can elicit the same response.

Zoo Piks International is a company that produces a wide variety of specialty swizzle sticks. Their tropical line of stirrers includes colorful palm trees, flamingos, sea horses and mermaids, while the southwestern line features plastic saguaros, rattlesnakes, barbed wire and howling coyotes. The Zoo Piks catalog makes for delightful reading.

Island Madness! is a firm that specializes in wild and wacky embellishments. Their imaginative line of swizzles includes everything from plastic Tiki heads and hula girls to pink elephants and tropical fish. The company is perhaps best known for their figural glass swizzles. These classy stirrers come in the hand-painted shapes of a toucan, pineapple, palm tree, flamingo, or parrot. They make great mementos of a lovely evening.

A bit more on the practical side are the rock candy swizzle sticks, the creation of Dryden & Palmer Rock Candy. The stirrers are an elegant alternative to using ordinary table sugar in specialty coffees and teas. The guests stir their drinks rendering the exact amount of sweetness desired.

Along the same lines are the chocolate truffle spoons made by Choco Pack. The company takes plastic spoons, scoops them full of delicious ganache truffle filling followed by a dip into Swiss chocolate. The finishing touch to these truffle spoons is an added dose of flavor—such as crème de menthe (mint), Kahlúa (coffee), Grand Marnier (orange), amaretto (almond), Chambord (black raspberry), or crème de cacao (chocolate). They add an unexpected touch of sophistication to a wide range of specialty drinks.

Garnishing

A drink's appearance has a dramatic impact on its perceived value. A garnish can make a drink more attractive and appetizing without significantly increasing its cost or raising the overall level of difficulty in preparation. Classic fruit garnishes are a good example.

Lime wedges are prepared by first cutting the fruit midway between the two ends. Laying the halves cut-side-down on a cutting board, quarter each half, totaling eight wedges per lime. Do not drop a lime wedge into a drink without first squeezing it. When squeezing a lime wedge, cup your other hand around it to shield people close by from being sprayed by the juice.

Lime, lemon and orange wheels are prepared by first making a shallow incision from one end of the fruit to the other, cutting just through the rind and slightly into the pulp. Next cut the entire fruit into quarter-inch-thick cross-sections. The smaller end slices can be discarded. The initial cut lengthwise creates a slit that allows the lime wheel to "sit" on the rim of a glass.

Lemon twists are prepared by removing the rind intact from the fruit and then cutting the rind into long, thin strips. But first, cut off each end of the lemon approximately 3/4" from the end. The citrus of the lemon should be fully exposed after these cuts.

Place the edge of a bar spoon (or the point of an ice pick or other sharp tool) between the rind and the fruit at either end of the lemon. Holding the lemon in the palm of one hand, turn it while gently pushing the tool slowly into the fruit. Continue until the tool emerges from the other end of the lemon. Then place the lemon on a cutting board and cut the rind end-to-end, removing the core of fruit. Flatten the rind without tearing it, cutting it into two narrower pieces if necessary. Cut 1/4"-wide strips from this flattened rind.

When using a lemon twist, hold the twist in both hands, with the thumbs on the white side and the tips of the index fingers on the yellow side. Aim the rind side of the lemon at the mouth of the glass and gently twist the peel. The twisting motion will cause the lemon to release its "essential oils," adding fragrance and flavor to a drink. Caution should be taken to not tear the rind. After twisting, drop the garnish into the drink.

CREAMY CHOCOLATE ALMOND

House specialty glass, chilled
Pour ingredients into blender
1 oz. orgeat (almond) syrup
2 oz. chocolate syrup
2 oz. Coco López Cream of Coconut
4 oz. milk
2-3 scoops vanilla ice cream
Blend ingredients
Whipped cream and drizzle
    chocolate syrup garnish

DREAMING OF MANGOES

House specialty glass, chilled
Pour ingredients into blender
3 oz. Frusia Mango Smoothie Base
6 oz. orange juice
Blend ingredients with ice
Top with 1 scoop mango
    or lemon sorbet
Lemon wheel garnish

FATS-NO DOMINO

House specialty glass, chilled
Pour ingredients into blender
6 oz. blueberry yogurt
1/2 oz. grenadine
1 oz. Torani Blueberry Syrup
4 oz. sweet 'n' sour
2-3 scoops lemon sorbet
Blend ingredients with ice
Splash lemon-lime soda
Lemon wheel garnish

FAUX MARGARITA

House specialty glass, ice
Rim glass with
    green-colored salt
*Pour ingredients into iced
    mixing glass*
3/4 oz. Rose's Lime Juice
1 oz. orange juice
1 oz. grapefruit juice
3 oz. margarita mix
3 oz. cold, brewed tea
Shake and strain
Lime wheel and wedge garnish

TORANI SPECIALTY FLAVORING SYRUPS

TORANI SPECIALTY FLAVORING SYRUPS were created for those who refuse to leave well enough alone. Renowned throughout the world for their exceptionally rich, true fruit flavors, Torani syrups have become the standard fare for those who believe that a little more flavor is a good thing.

R. Torre & Company began in 1925 when founders Rinaldo and Ezilda Torre set out to create authentic Italian syrups based on the old-world recipes they brought from Lucca, Italy. The couple perfected five traditional flavoring syrups, which soon became local favorites in San Francisco's Italian neighborhood.

Torani Specialty Syrups are made from all-natural flavor extracts imported from around the world and expertly blended to achieve the most authentic flavor possible. They are low fat and entirely alcohol-free.

The famous Torani line now contains over 60 brilliant flavoring syrups. They range in diversity from pink grapefruit, passion fruit and Mandarin orange to hazelnut, root beer and watermelon. There are even five varieties of chocolate.

Singular to the Torani line are such specialties as Almond Roca®, a re-creation of the famous candy in syrup form, Chocolate Biscotti, a syrup with a bakery-fresh flavor of the traditional, crisp Italian cookie, Tiramisu, a syrup that captures the delectable flavor of the famed Italian dessert, and date-flavored Tamarindo, one of the five original syrups.

Torani syrups are used to flavor everything from lattes, cappuccinos and hot cocoa drinks to iced teas, milkshakes and lemonades.

FRANCO'S COLORED MARGARITA SALT

Imagine devising a fabulous alcohol-free margarita only to be faced with the prospect of sending it out in public dressed in a rim of ordinary salt. It's too pedestrian for a true work of art. Fear not, the fashion police at Franco's have solved the dilemma of the under-dressed margarita once and for all. They have created a line of designer salts and sugars that lend an air of sophistication and taste to a wide range of specialties.

Franco's Colored Margarita Salt is a welcome innovation. The coloring is permanently adhered to the salt so it won't run or bleed and its taste is unaffected. The line includes ten festive, brightly colored salts, including blue, green, orange, gold, pink, purple, red, turquoise and yellow. Franco's has also perfected a lime green, citrus-flavored salt.

Imagine the possibilities of alcohol-free margaritas and Bloody Marys with the variety of these colored salts. Different colors can be assigned to different specialty drinks, or the salt colors can be mixed together. Add a few pinches of the citrus-flavored salt and the creative possibilities are almost unlimited.

The company has also made fashion news with Franco's Colored Rimming Sugars. The diverse line includes red, yellow, orange, gold and purple, as well as the flavors of raspberry, lemon, cherry, peach and watermelon. The various colors and flavors can be mixed, making them ideal complements to a wide variety of alcohol-free specialties. For an entirely different presentation, rim the edge of a glass first with grenadine before dipping it into Franco's colored sugar.

FAUX BERRY-RITA

House specialty glass, ice
Rim glass with Franco's Blue Margarita Salt
Pour ingredients into iced mixing glass
3/4 oz. Rose's Lime Juice
3 oz. margarita mix
3 oz. cold, brewed tea
3 oz. Frusia Raspberry Smoothie Base
Shake and strain
Lime wheel and wedge garnish

FLYING V BERRY COLADA

House specialty glass, chilled
Pour ingredients into blender
1 cup strawberries, fresh or frozen
1 oz. chocolate syrup
2 oz. Coco López Cream of Coconut
3 oz. pineapple juice
2-3 scoops vanilla ice cream
Blend ingredients
Whipped cream and strawberry garnish

HANGOVER-FREE BANANA MARGARITA

House specialty glass, chilled
Rim glass with Franco's
   Yellow-Colored Sugar
Pour ingredients into blender
1/2 banana, peeled
3/4 oz. fresh lime juice
1 oz. orange juice
2 oz. True Crystals Banana Daiquiri Mix
4 oz. margarita mix
Blend ingredients with ice
Lime wheel and banana slice garnish

HARVEST PUNCH

Punch bowl, ice
Build in punch bowl
6 oz. Torani
   Peach Syrup
6 oz. Torani Blackberry
   Syrup
20 oz. apple cider
28 oz. cold, brewed tea
24 oz. prep. lemonade
1 liter club soda
Float lime, lemon and
   orange wheels
Makes 12-18 servings

HERBA BUENA

House specialty glass, ice
Rim glass with Franco's Lime Green
   Citrus Margarita Salt
Pour ingredients into mixing glass
5-6 mint leaves
1/2 oz. simple syrup
1/2 orange wheel
Muddle contents
Add ice
1/2 oz. Rose's Lime Juice
3/4 oz. fresh lime juice
3/4 oz. orange juice
4 oz. margarita mix
4 oz. cold, brewed tea, sweetened
Shake and strain
Lime wedge and mint sprig garnish

JAMOCHA COLADA

House specialty glass, chilled
Pour ingredients into blender
1 cup Dole Pineapple Chunks
2 oz. Coco López Cream of Coconut
1 oz. coffee syrup
2 oz. pineapple juice
2 oz. cold, brewed coffee
2-3 scoops vanilla ice cream
Blend ingredients
Whipped cream, pineapple wedge
   and drizzle chocolate syrup garnish

LUPITA WITH SANGRITA

House specialty glass, ice
Rim glass with
   red-colored salt
Pour ingredients into blender
3/4 oz. Rose's Lime Juice
1/4 jalapeño pepper, diced
1/2 cup mango, diced
1/2 tsp. chile powder
1/2 tsp. red onion, diced
1 tsp. cilantro, chopped
4-6 dashes pepper sauce
1 garlic clove, crushed
2 oz. orange juice
6 oz. tomato juice
Blend ingredients
Lemon and lime wheel garnish

ROSE'S® SWEETENED LIME JUICE

In 1865, Lauchlin Rose founded L. Rose & Company in Leith, Scotland. Shortly after, the British Royal Navy approached Rose about creating a lime juice. Sailors needed the ascorbic acid in fruits such as limes to ward off the debilitating effects of scurvy. At first, a small amount of rum was used to preserve ROSE'S SWEETENED LIME JUICE. In 1867, Rose developed and patented a process for preserving fresh lime juice without the use of alcohol.

Rose's Lime Juice continues to be the best selling lime juice in the world. It is made from fresh limes grown on Dominica, one of the Caribbean Windward Islands, as well as those cultivated on the company's lime plantations in Ghana.

Why use Rose's Lime Juice in drinks instead of fresh lime juice? While there is a cache to using fresh limes, inconsistency can be a reoccurring problem. Sometimes the limes available in markets are sweet and juicy, other times they're small, hard and relatively bitter, making them wholly inappropriate for use in drink making. Rose's Lime Juice, on the other hand, is a constant.

It is light-bodied and delightfully tart. A dose of Rose's in an alcohol-free cocktail adds a refreshing splash of lime flavor without the slightest trace of bitterness, an attribute ideal for mixologists.

The company also makes another indispensable product for behind the bar, Rose's Grenadine Syrup. It is one of only a few grenadines on the market with an authentic pomegranate taste and a finish that is flavorful without being cloying.

COCO LÓPEZ
CREAM OF COCONUT

While objects of affection for centuries, coconuts are quite the contradiction. How can something so delicious be so incredibly difficult to eat? Cracking the mysteries of the coconut became the professional pursuit of Don Ramon López Irizarry. Working in a small laboratory in Puerto Rico, López mastered the process of blending the cream from the tender meat of Caribbean coconuts with precisely the right amount of pure cane sugar to create a thoroughly smooth and creamy product.

The result of his efforts is the classic COCO LÓPEZ CREAM OF COCONUT. Made according to the original 1950s recipe, the coconut cream has become a fixture in mixology for good reasons. It has a luxuriously rich body capable of transforming a drink from weak to broad shouldered. The mix also has an amazingly authentic coconut flavor, one surprisingly free of sweetness.

Coco López Cream of Coconut was most assuredly present when the piña colada was created in 1954 at the Caribe Hilton in San Juan. It is one of the ingredients that literally defines the drink. The remarkably thick and silky syrup is aromatic and loaded with enough flavor to shine even when highly diluted.

Coco López is the featured coconut performer in scores of delicious alcohol-free recipes. It easily mixes with most types of juice—most notably pineapple—as well as ice cream, sherbet and sorbet.

The company has developed several other offerings, including Coco López Piña Colada Mix and Coco López Coconut Milk, an exotic treat once only available in the tropics.

ORANGE COCONUT FROST
House specialty glass, chilled
Pour ingredients into blender
3 oz. orange juice concentrate
6 oz. sweet 'n' sour
1/8 tsp. vanilla extract
1 banana, peeled
2 1/2 oz. Coco López Cream of Coconut
Blend ingredients with ice
Whipped cream garnish

ROCA MOCHA GRANITA
House specialty glass, chilled
Pour ingredients into blender
1 oz. Torani Almond Roca® Syrup
1 oz. Torani Crème de Cacao Syrup
1/2 oz. Torani French Vanilla Syrup
4 oz. cold espresso
6 oz. 2% milk
Blend ingredients with ice
Whipped cream garnish

ROYALE FRAMBOISE
House specialty glass, chilled
Pour ingredients into blender
1 oz. raspberry syrup
1/2 cup raspberries, fresh or frozen
2 oz. Coco López Cream of Coconut
4 oz. sweet 'n' sour
3-4 scoops vanilla ice cream
Blend ingredients
Whipped cream and drizzle
   chocolate syrup garnish

TROPICAL
BREEZE SPRITZER
House specialty
   glass, chilled
*Pour ingredients
   into blender*
1/2 cup papaya, cubed
1/2 banana, peeled
1 oz. Coco López
   Cream of Coconut
4 oz. tropical juice blend
2-3 scoops vanilla ice cream
Blend ingredients
Splash club soda
Pineapple wedge garnish

No Longer 5¢ a Glass, Lemonade Has Gone Uptown

Lemonade is one of America's favorite drinks. No longer restricted to spring and summer, lemonade is now popularly consumed throughout the year. The secret to its success lies in its naturally refreshing nature and the delicious balance it strikes between sweet and tart.

While it's easy to perceive lemonade as an American invention, its origins actually predate the founding of this country. Historical records suggest that lemonade originated in France in the early 1600s. Sugar prices had dropped dramatically, allowing for expanded uses, such as the sweetening of local fruit. Merchants were soon steeping lemons in water and sugar, selling the mixture at inns and taverns.

By the mid-1760s, fleets of vendors with large vessels strapped to their backs roamed the streets of Paris selling lemonade by the cup to the city's parched citizenry. It wasn't long before lemonade became a popular treat throughout Provence and Italy.

The widespread cultivation of lemons in the United States took off with advancements in irrigation, which by the early 1900s, helped turn vast, barren tracts of Florida and California into some of the world's most prolific farmland. By that time, railroads connected most of the country, allowing growers to distribute citrus nationwide using refrigerated cars.

From roadside stands and ballparks to restaurants and hotels, lemonade changed America's taste forever. It has become a part of our national psyche. Lemonade and good times are inseparable concepts. In this country, the answer to "Would you like a glass of lemonade?" is a given.

Creating Lemonade Classics

Making great lemonade should be a requirement of citizenship. Possibly the most bankable recipe for homemade lemonade is a recipe that actually belongs to someone's Great Granny. At the onset, it's important to understand that this is not the quick method of preparing lemonade. It begins by immersing 5-6 large lemons in a bowl with near boiling water for about 2 minutes. Pour off the water and let the lemons cool several minutes. Once they have sufficiently cooled, roll the lemons dry on a towel, releasing their juices in the process. Taking care not to lose any juice, cut the lemon into thin slices and layer them in a mixing bowl. Sprinkle each successive layer with sugar and occasionally press the fruit with a wooden spoon. This should be done gently so as not to break up the pulp. After the lemons have been sliced and sugared, the mixture should sit for about 30 minutes.

Transfer the entire contents of the bowl into a large pitcher and add 3 quarts of cold spring water. Stir the mixture and let stand in the refrigerator to allow the mixture to become fully integrated. Serve in a tall, iced glass with a fresh lemon wedge.

While lemonade may essentially be little more than lemon juice, sugar and water, it would be a pity to dismiss it as a simple, uninvolved concoction. Like any great beverage, it has nuances to be fathomed and numerous creative applications to explore. The following should prove the point.

Lemon Facts — Like all citrus, the skins of lemons have pores through which the fruit can lose moisture. To prevent this, growers add a thin layer of wax. It is advisable to soak the fruit in boiling water to remove the wax prior to use. The process will also make the lemons juicier.

One medium-sized lemon will yield about 1/4 cup of juice and 2 teaspoons of zest. When selecting lemons, pick yellow-skinned fruit over those with green skins and choose according to weight not size. Heavier lemons contain more juice. Before slicing the fruit, roll them on a hard surface. This should increase how much juice is obtained.

Lemon juice can be maintained frozen for long periods of time. One creative option is to freeze it in ice cube trays. The juice can then be added at a later time to various mixed drinks or used in the preparation of lemonade. Along the same lines, slightly thawed lemonade concentrate can be used in numerous punches and specialty concoctions.

Preparation Tips — The largest ingredient in lemonade is water, so choose wisely. Tap water may have off-flavors not necessarily well suited for use in drink making. Distilled water will provide a neutral base, while spring water will add the subtle flavor of minerals. One refreshing option is to make lemonade with sparkling water instead of still.

Sweetening lemonade is made easier using simple syrup instead of granulated sugar. To make the syrup, bring 2 cups of water to a boil and add in an equal amount of sugar. When it cools, the sugar will remain in solution. Simple syrup will prevent the problem of undissolved granulated sugar settling to the bottom of a glass.

Pink Lemonade — According to *Ripley's Believe It or Not*, pink lemonade was invented in 1857 by Pete

Conklin who unwittingly used water from a bucket in which a circus performer had soaked his red tights. Thankfully, pink lemonade is now made by adding in a splash of red grape juice, or alternatively cranberry juice.

Limeade — Sweetened lime juice can easily be as delicious and refreshing as lemonade. Fresh limes are notoriously inconsistent, however. Sometimes they're sweet and juicy, other times they border on bitter. For best results, start with a known entity, such as ReaLime Lime Juice, True Crystals Tart Lime Mixer, or Freshies Lime Margarita Mix.

Creative Variations — The flavor of lemonade is complemented by an array of other tastes making it a nearly universal mixer. One notable example is making lemonade with equal parts of lime juice and lemon juice. The balance of flavors is singularly refreshing. The crowning touch is adding a splash of grapefruit juice and/or orange juice to the lemon/lime mix. It rounds out the citrus palate and adds intriguing dimension to the aroma.

Armed with Torani syrups there's no limit on what can be created within a glass of lemonade. The citrus base marries beautifully with the taste of blueberry, raspberry, pineapple, strawberry, kiwi, watermelon, pomegranate, or grape, just to name a few of the flavors that Torani has mastered. Start the lemonade with some fresh fruit on the bottom of the glass and finish with it as a garnish.

Lemonade is often served with an equal portion of iced tea—popularly known as an Arnold Palmer—or blended with ice and served as a slushy. It can be sweetened with honey and flavored with mint. For an interesting blast of effervescence, try adding in a splash of ginger ale or ginger beer, or for that matter, add some Martinelli's Sparkling Apple Cider.

Lemonade Floats are a savory treat. They are easily prepared by adding a scoop of lemon sorbet to a 3/4 full glass of lemonade. Of course there's no reason to limit oneself to a solitary flavor of sorbet when so many exist. Consider also using lime or raspberry sorbet, but mandarin orange or passion fruit sorbet are also marvelous additions.

A Tropical Julep is a delectable variation of the All-American lemonade. To a pitcher containing 6-7 sprigs of mint, add equal parts of lemon and grapefruit juice to a base of white grape juice. Mix in some grated fresh pineapple and refrigerate for about 30 minutes allowing the concoction to fully steep. Serve in tall, iced glasses and finish with a splash of ginger ale and a lemon slice garnish.

REALEMON® LEMON JUICE

REALEMON LEMON JUICE was introduced in 1934 and its sister product, REALIME® LIME JUICE, debuted during World War II. By the 1950s, the tandem products had become the brand food and beverage professionals relied on. There are three, rock solid reasons why.

ReaLemon and ReaLime are unaffected by seasonality, and ounce for ounce, they are more economical than hand squeezed fruit. It is clearly more convenient using ReaLemon or ReaLime juice in food preparation or drink making and foregoing the hassle of juicing. Finally, each is a more consistent commodity than freshly squeezed juice.

Both ReaLemon and ReaLime are made by concentrating the juice of high quality fresh lemons and limes. Water is then added to reconstitute them back to the strength of natural juice. The lemons used are cultivated in the United States and Argentina, while the fresh limes are grown in Brazil and Mexico.

Of the three reasons why these brands are preeminent, none carries more importance to working professionals than consistency. Purchasing fresh citrus can be an "iffy" proposition. Often, especially when not in season, lemons and limes can be excessively tart and bitter. Working with a blended concentrate allows the company to produce a juice with a balanced taste profile.

ReaLemon and ReaLime have the look of real juice because they are 100% real juice. They are loaded with robust bouquets and zesty, citrusy flavor. Both products are ideally suited for use in alcohol-free specialty drinks, such as margaritas, iced teas, daiquiris and lemonades.

FLOATING ICEBERG LEMONADE

House specialty glass, chilled
Build in glass
2-3 scoops lemon sherbet
1/2 fill prepared lemonade
1/2 fill club soda
Lemon wheel garnish

FRECKLED MARTIAN LEMONADE

House specialty glass, chilled
Rim glass with green-colored salt
Pour ingredients into blender
8 oz. prepared lemonade
3 kiwi, peeled and sliced
3/4 oz. Rose's Lime Juice
Blend ingredients with ice
Kiwi slice garnish

FRUITY SUMMER SLUSH LEMONADE

House specialty glass, chilled
Pour ingredients into blender
1 cup strawberries, fresh or frozen
1/2 cup watermelon, cubed
6 oz. prepared lemonade
1 tbs. sugar
Blend ingredients with ice
Strawberry garnish

ISLAND GUAVA LEMONADE

House specialty glass, chilled
Pour ingredients into blender
3 oz. Island Oasis Guava Beverage Mix
6 oz. prepared lemonade
Blend ingredients with ice
Lemon wheel garnish

LEMONADE SPARKLER

House specialty glass, ice
Build in glass
8 oz. Martinelli Sparkling Cider
4 oz. prepared lemonade
Lemon wheel and mint leaf garnish

LUAU LEMONADE

House specialty glass, chilled
Pour ingredients into blender
1 cup pineapple chunks
1 tsp. confectioner's sugar
1 oz. raspberry syrup
6 oz. prepared lemonade
Blend ingredients with ice
Splash club soda
Lemon wheel garnish

MANGO LEMONADE

House specialty glass, ice
Pour ingredients into iced mixing glass
4 oz. mango puree
2 oz. orange juice
6 oz. True Crystals Lemonade Mix
Shake and strain
Orange wheel garnish

POMEGRANATE LEMONADE

House specialty glass, ice
Pour ingredients into iced mixing glass
1 oz. grenadine
8 oz. prepared lemonade
Shake and strain
Lemon wheel garnish

PRETTY IN PINK LEMONADE

House specialty glass, ice
Pour ingredients into iced mixing glass
1 oz. raspberry syrup
8 oz. prepared lemonade
2 oz. cranberry juice
Shake and strain
Lemon wheel and strawberry garnish

QUICK-DRAW LEMONADE

House specialty glass, ice
Pour ingredients into iced mixing glass
1 oz. Torani Ginger Spice Syrup
8 oz. prepared lemonade
Shake and strain
Fill with ginger ale
Lemon wheel garnish

TRUE CRYSTALS® LEMONADE MIXER

There is a certain cachet to making lemonade using fresh, tree-ripened fruit. Those with the time, inclination and availability of a case of fresh lemons will be rewarded with a great glass of lemonade.

For those of us who crave only the result and not the process, TRUE CRYSTALS® LEMONADE MIXER is indeed a marvelous innovation. It is made using fresh lemon juice. The lemon juice is freeze-dried using patented technology to capture the pure, natural flavor of the fruit. The enhanced granules reconstitute to their natural state with the addition of water. Preparation time takes about a minute.

The result is a marvelously appealing lemonade. It has good color, brilliant clarity and is pulp-free. The mixer has a light citrusy bouquet and a classic, lemony finish. The lemonade is a delicious, well-balanced treat.

The company also makes True Crystals® Limeade Mixer. As the name would imply, it is made using real lime juice, sweetened and freeze-dried into crystals. It is brimming with vitality and has scores of applications behind the bar, none more savory than adding it to lemonade. As naturally complementary flavors, limeade and lemonade marry together into something wonderfully refreshing.

Both of the True Crystals® mixers are first rate and ideally suited for anyone looking for a delectable, consistent product who isn't interested in squeezing lemons or limes by the case.

RAZZLE DAZZLE LIMEADE
House specialty glass, chilled
Build in glass
1 scoop lemon sherbet
1 scoop raspberry sherbet
6 oz. prepared limeade
Fill with lemon-lime soda
Strawberry garnish

RED, WHITE AND
BLUE LEMONADE
House specialty glass, chilled
Build in glass
2 cherries
2 blueberries
1/2 oz. raspberry syrup
1-2 scoops vanilla ice cream
8 oz. True Crystals Lemonade Mix
Splash club soda
Float 1 oz. blueberry syrup
Whipped cream, cherry
   and blueberry garnish

SMURFY LEMONADE
House specialty glass, ice
Pour ingredients into iced mixing glass
8 oz. prepared lemonade
1 1/2 oz. blueberry syrup
Shake and strain
Lemon wheel garnish

BATCH RECIPES

HOMEMADE LEMONADE
Large pitcher, ice
Combine ingredients in large saucepan
2 cups sugar
2 cups water
Heat to near boil. Stir until clear, let cool.

Add ingredients
2 cups fresh lemon juice
7 cups water
1/2 tsp. finely grated lemon peel
Stir thoroughly and chill before serving
Serve in large pitcher filled with ice
Makes 8-10 servings

HOMEMADE LIMEADE
Large pitcher, ice
Combine ingredients in large saucepan
2 cups sugar
2 cups water
Heat to near boil. Stir until clear, let cool.

Add ingredients
2 cups fresh lime juice
7 cups water
1/2 tsp. finely grated lime peel
Stir thoroughly and chill before serving
Serve in large pitcher filled with ice
Makes 8-10 servings

INDIAN-STYLE LEMONADE
Large pitcher, ice
Combine ingredients in large pitcher
8 cups water
1/2 cup ReaLime Lime Juice
2/3 cup ReaLemon Lemon Juice
1 1/3 cups maple syrup
1 tsp. ground ginger
1/8 tsp. cayenne pepper (optional)
Stir ingredients
Mint sprig garnish
Makes 6-8 servings

PINEAPPLE-LEMON PUNCH
Punch bowl
Step 1: Make punch syrup
Combine ingredients in large saucepan
   3 cups pineapple juice
   3 lemons, juiced
   1 cup white sugar
   1/2 cup honey
   Over medium heat, bring to a boil,
      stirring frequently and cook for
      one minute. Allow to cool, then
      refrigerate over night.
Step 2: Make Punch
Combine ingredients in punch bowl
   1/2 fill punch bowl with ice
   Add 2 liters club soda
   Add chilled punch syrup
   Add 1 lemon, lime and
      orange, thinly sliced
Lime leaves garnish
Makes 6-8 servings

Chapter 8

Popping the Top
Off the World of Sodas

They are effervescent, flavorful and Americans love them. Sodas have become an integral part of everyday life in this country. Imagine an office building or public venue without access to a soda vending machine. Not a chance.

The interesting question is how did sodas become so deeply rooted in the cultural fabric of the nation? After all, regardless of the brand name on the label, soda pops are all essentially the same thing, artificially charged, water-based mixtures with flavorings of some sort. What is it about these carbonated drinks that has made them America's drink of choice?

A partial explanation can be traced to such famous European spas as Vichy, Evian, San Pelligrino and Perrier, where for centuries people have sought out their mineral waters for the rejuvenating effects. These naturally effervescent waters were seen as curatives with healing and revitalizing powers. Eventually these waters were bottled and made available throughout the continent.

In 1772, British scientist Joseph Priestly became the first to successfully produce artificially carbonated water. He produced the carbonated waters in barrels, flavored them with lime juice for use by the Royal Navy to prevent sailors from contracting scurvy. By 1793, Jacob Schweppe began bottling soda water, or seltzer as it became known. It was considered a patent remedy and often contained medicinal herbs and elixirs. After that, bottled mineral waters, spring waters and manufactured seltzers flourished.

The realm of carbonated beverages changed forever with the creation of Coca-Cola in 1886. Dr. John Pemberton, a pharmacist in Atlanta, created a proprietary flavored syrup in his back yard, which when mixed in carbonated water, became a good tasting restorative. At first, the fountain drink was intended solely for the customers at his pharmacy's soda fountain, but less than ten years later, Coca-Cola was being bottled and had become available in every state in the Union.

Many other types of beverages, however, have made a splash in the United States only to fall out of fashion a short time later. Why have sodas flourished and enjoyed enormous popularity in this country for more than a century?

It's all about lifestyle. Sodas are consumed anytime of day by just about every segment of the population—kids, adults, rich and poor. They are relatively inexpensive and provide a flavorful, effervescent break in the day. Sodas can be found at almost any type of occasion and celebration. They are drunk at picnics and sporting events, at the movies and in the car. The 1928 Coca-Cola slogan summarized it best; sodas are truly "The Pause that Refreshes."

Soda Waters Become Pop Culture

Today, the field of entrants is still largely dominated by brands such as Coke, Pepsi, Seven-Up, Canada Dry Ginger Ale, Hires Root Beer and Dr. Pepper. But catering to a soda-gulping nation requires more than offering the standard bill of fare. The tried-and-true brands have become successful for good reason, yet there are many smaller, boutique lines of soda that are new, fresh and exciting.

Making serious strides with soda enthusiasts are more of these avant-garde pops.

Skeleteens — It should come as no surprise that the one of the wackiest, zaniest line of sodas has its origins in southern California. With names such as Brain Wash, Love Potion #69 and Black Lemonade, Skeleteens are great tasting, herbal-based sodas that boggle the imagination.

These aren't kiddy sodas in any respect. The skull and crossbones on the Brain Wash and Black Lemonade labels, or the skeleton hand ripping into a heart on the Love Potion #69 label are your first clues that these are adult-oriented sodas. Skeleteens don't taste like conventional sodas either. Made with herbs such as ginseng, ginko biloba, skull cap, jalapeño, ginger, gotu cola, mad dog weed, capsicum and a truck load of caffeine, Skeleteens are downright zippy, and guaranteed to get your motor running.

Real Soda — Founded in Rancho Palos Verdes, California in 1991, Real Sodas are decidedly cutting edge products. The company offers such sodas as KavaKaze, a sparkling herbal soda made with kavakava, guarana, ginseng, ginko biloba, capsicum and green tea, Rejuvenizer, a green tea and cranberry herbal soda, Electrolizer, an herbal recovery drink loaded with electrolytes, vitamins and amino acids, and Africola, a power cola sold in a bottle shaped like a penguin. Real Sodas are delicious and arguably good for the physiology.

Blue Sky — Made in Santa Fe, New Mexico since 1983, Blue Sky sodas are all-natural beverages containing no preservatives, additives or artificial colors, flavors, or caffeine. The line of outstanding sodas includes Premium Ginseng, Cherry Vanilla, Raspberry, Grape, Truly Orange, Jamaican Ginger Ale and Grapefruit.

Borgnine's — For many people, Borgnine's Coffee Soda is the best of both worlds. This Californian soda is microbrewed made from Italian roast coffee. It has layers of sweetened cola and coffee flavors all interlaced with a shot of caffeine. The soda is something special. And it's made by the daughter of actor Ernest Borgnine, giving it celebrity status.

 Willie's Hemp Sodas — Founded in 1994, Willie's makes energizing and revitalizing sodas that don't contain caffeine, sodium, or dyes. Willie's Ginger Hemp Soda is made from ginger oil, hemp seed oil and ginseng. The Hemp line of sodas also includes Butterscotch, Black Cherry, Wild Citrus and Root Beer.

 Sprecher — Made in Milwaukee at the Sprecher Brewing Company, the line of small batch sodas are made in gas-fired brew kettles combining honey, vanilla and an array of aromatic botanicals. The sodas are outstanding, full-flavored and loaded with character. The line includes Orange Dream, Ginger Ale and Ravin' Red, a pop made with Wisconsin cherry and cranberry juice, honey and ginseng. Sprecher sodas are available by the 1/2 and 1/4 barrel.

 Thomas Kemper Sodas — Thomas Kemper is a nationally acclaimed micro-brewery on Bainbridge Island on Puget Sound. When the master brewer isn't concocting world class beer, he's engaged making world class sodas. The line is outstanding and includes Vanilla Cream, Classic Grape, Black Cherry, Orange Cream, Ginger Ale and Root Beer, the brewery's leading attraction.

Creating Soda Pop Classics

One of the best uses for a scoop of vanilla ice cream is dropping it into a tall, frosted mug of root beer. It may be one of the finest things that can be drunk through a straw. The melting of flavors and textures, the melding of cold, creamy ice cream and frothy root beer make the Root Beer Float a sublime experience.

Fortunately for all of us, there are no plausible limitations to what is possible when ice cream and sodas are mixed. Borgnine's Coffee Soda was destined to be married with ice cream. It's a float that works with any number of flavors of ice cream.

Creativity rules the day when it comes to making soda-based drinks. The Skeleteens Black Lemonade is perfect paired with lemon sorbet. Raspberry sorbet can be featured with a hearty black cherry soda, while vanilla cream sodas have met their soul mate in chocolate ice cream. Experiment, have fun and enrich the lives of others.

Italian sodas are a popular attraction in bistros and cafés. Part of their joy is in their simplicity. Italian sodas are made with ice, soda water and a float of one or more Torani syrups. The delicate flavoring dissolves immediately into the seltzer, transforming it into a marvelously light soda. The Torani line is so diverse and broad that there are unlimited creative possibilities. Whether it is made with a single flavor such as raspberry, or a combination such as kiwi/lime, watermelon/blueberry or coffee/chocolate, Italian sodas can be an incomparable treat.

JONES SODA M.F. GRAPE

The Jones Soda Company has turned a lot of heads since its inception in 1995. They burst onto the contemporary beverage scene sporting an innovative line of wildly flavored brands such as M.F. Grape, Green Apple and Berry Lemonade.

JONES SODA M.F. GRAPE is an excellent example of how refreshing and cutting edge these trend-setting sodas are. A twist on the traditional grape soda, Jones gave their lively version of this classic pop an amethyst purple color, wafting grape aroma and a delicate, long-lasting grape flavor.

All of the Jones Sodas are refreshing and completely in-step with today's tastes. For instance, the turquoise colored Berry Lemonade has a subtle blueberry aroma and a blue raspberry flavor with a lingering lemony finish. Jones Green Apple is fluorescent green and has the delicious, sweet/tart taste of freshly cut green apples.

For a small company, Jones has a rather extensive offering of sodas. In addition to such classics as root beer, cherry and cream soda, the line also includes Crushed Melon, Strawberry Lime, Blue Bubblegum, Vanilla Cola, Fufu Berry and Orange Cream.

Jones has also created a non-carbonated natural drink line, for those who are health-conscious or simply want a great tasting drink. Featured in the line are Bada Bing!, cherry and loganberry; Dave, green tea with hemp; and Berry White, strawberry, cherry and grapefruit juice.

Don't expect to see your favorite Jones Soda with the same label for more than a short while. They change the look of their labels as often as most of us change our socks.

CAPTAIN MARVEL

House specialty glass, ice
Pour ingredients into iced mixing glass
3/4 oz. grenadine
1 oz. grapefruit juice
2 oz. orange juice
2 oz. cranberry juice
Shake and strain
Fill with Squirt
Lemon wedge garnish

CHOCOLATE CHERRY COLA

House specialty glass, chilled
Build in glass
2 tbs. chocolate syrup
3 oz. cola
6 oz. whole milk
Stir contents gently
Add 1 scoop vanilla ice cream
Whipped cream and drizzle cherry syrup garnish with Oreo and vanilla wafer cookie

COFFEE HAZELNUT FLOAT

House specialty glass, chilled
Pour ingredients into blender
1 oz. hazelnut syrup
1-2 scoops vanilla ice cream
1-2 scoops coffee ice cream
4 oz. cold, brewed coffee
Blend ingredients
Fill with club soda
Whipped cream and drizzle coffee syrup garnish

CONQUERED GRAPE

House specialty glass, ice
Rim glass with red-colored sugar
Pour ingredients into iced mixing glass
1/2 oz. cherry syrup
1/2 oz. strawberry syrup
2 oz. sweet 'n' sour
2 oz. Concord grape juice
Shake and strain
Fill with cola
Orange wheel and cherry garnish

COZY CHOCO BELLY

House specialty glass, chilled
Build in glass
3 oz. cold, brewed coffee
1 scoop chocolate ice cream
1 scoop vanilla ice cream
1 oz. chocolate syrup
Fill with cola
Whipped cream and
    powdered cocoa garnish

CUPID'S CLOUD SODA

House specialty glass, chilled
Rim glass with red-colored sugar
Pour ingredients into blender
4-6 strawberries
1 tbs. strawberry preserves
3-4 scoops vanilla ice cream
5 oz. ginger ale
Blend ingredients
Sugar-coated strawberry garnish

DOWNTOWN ROOT BEER

House specialty glass, chilled
Pour ingredients into iced mixing glass
1 oz. chocolate syrup
2 oz. whole milk
2 oz. sweet 'n' sour
Shake and strain
Add 2-3 scoops vanilla ice cream
Fill with root beer
Whipped cream and Oreo garnish

DREAMY APPLE
SPRITZER

House specialty glass, chilled
Rim glass with
    green-colored sugar
Pour ingredients into blender
1/2 oz. Rose's Lime Juice
4 oz. apple juice
3-4 scoops vanilla ice cream
Blend ingredients
Fill with lemon-lime soda
Cherry garnish

SHASTA MANGO SODA

The Shasta Mineral Springs Company was formed in 1889 to bottle the sparkling spring waters at the Shasta Health Resort in California. In the 1920s, the company expanded its line to include flavored soft drinks, and they've remained among the most enduring beverage brand.

Among the many decisions the company has made over the decades, none seem better than creating a line of sodas specifically targeting the tastes of Hispanics. Today, they are the fastest growing population segment in the country and they have a friend in Shasta.

The flagship of the highly successful line is SHASTA MANGO SODA, a delectable, tangerine-colored pop. The mildly effervescent and impressively aromatic soda has a true-to-fruit flavor. It is easy-to-drink and a guaranteed crowd-pleaser.

The other Hispanic-oriented sodas include Shasta Jamaica, a scarlet, deliciously tart drink made from the hibiscus flower, Manzana, a red apple flavored soda, and Horchata, a semi-sweet beverage with a taste closely resembling rice pudding. Thirst-quenching Zázz is flavored with lime and grapefruit and Tamarindo is made from the tangy fruit of the tamarind tree.

The Shasta portfolio also features Cascadia, savory, sparkling waters flavored with fruit juice, only 2 calories each. Unlike some other sparkling waters, Cascadia delivers on its promise of flavor. The line includes Orange Mango, Raspberry Black Currant, Pink Grapefruit and Lemonade.

If two calories are too many, try Cascadia Sparkling Clear, a family of calorie-free, caffeine-free sodas in a wide array of interesting, and in some cases, exotic flavors.

EGG CREAM REVISITED

House specialty glass, ice
Pour ingredients into iced mixing glass
3 oz. whole milk
2 oz. whipped cream
2 oz. chocolate syrup
Shake and strain
Fill with club soda
Whipped cream and drizzle
    chocolate syrup garnish

FLORIDA KEYS FLOAT

House specialty glass, chilled
Build in glass
2-3 strawberries, sliced
3-4 half-moon orange slices
1/4 oz. fresh lime juice
1/4 oz. fresh lemon juice
2-3 scoops lemon sherbet
Fill with Shasta Mango Soda
Lime and lemon wheels garnish

ITALIAN CREAM SODA

House specialty glass, ice
Pour ingredients into iced mixing glass
3/4 oz. Torani Passion Fruit Syrup
3/4 oz. Torani Watermelon Syrup
1 oz. half & half cream
Shake and strain
Fill with club soda
Strawberry garnish

LEMON CREAM SODA

House specialty glass, ice
Build in glass
1 oz. lemon syrup
1/2 oz. vanilla syrup
3/4 oz. half & half cream
Fill with club soda
Lemon wheel garnish

MISS GEORGIA MIST

House specialty glass, crushed ice
Build in glass
3/4 oz. peach syrup
1/2 oz. lime syrup
Fill with lemon-lime soda
Lime wedge garnish

PINK MANIFESTO

House specialty glass, chilled
Pour ingredients into blender
1/2 oz. grenadine
1 oz. cranberry juice
1 oz. prepared lemonade
1 1/2 oz. orange juice
2 oz. pineapple juice
Blend ingredients with ice
Fill with ginger ale
Orange wedge garnish

POWDER PUFF'S
SWEAT BUCKET

House specialty glass, chilled
Build in glass
6 oz. Jones Soda M.F. Grape
6 oz. Squirt
1 scoop vanilla ice cream
Orange wheel, cherries and red licorice
    drizzle blueberry syrup garnish

ROYAL CINCINNATI

House specialty glass, ice
Build in glass
2 oz. orange soda
2 oz. cola
2 oz. root beer
2 oz. lemon-lime soda
Fill with prepared lemonade
Lemon wedge garnish

SEAWEED GROG

House specialty glass, ice
Build in glass
1/2 oz. Rose's Lime Juice
2 oz. orange juice
2 oz. sweet 'n' sour
Fill with ginger ale
Orange wheel garnish

SICILIAN SPLASH

House specialty glass, ice
Build in glass
2 oz. orange soda
4 oz. white grape juice
Fill with club soda
Lemon wedge garnish

Chapter 9

Effervescent or Not, Apple Cider is Pressed for Success

No other fruit is more chronicled in history than the apple. There is evidence that apples were eaten during the Stone Age in Europe and along the Nile River Delta as early as 1300 BC. Apples existed during the halcyon days of the Greek Republic and Roman Empire. When Julius Caesar invaded England in 55 BC, he found the villagers in Kent produced a beverage from apples called cider. Then there's the incident involving William Tell being forced to shoot an apple off the head of his son.

Apples existed in America years before the arrival of the Pilgrims. Unfortunately for the settlers they were the crabapple variety and unusable for cider. The Massachusetts Bay Colony requested seeds and cuttings from England, which were brought over on later voyages of the Mayflower. People from other European countries immigrating into the United States included apple seeds among their provisions. Well before the founding of the original 13 colonies, apples were being cultivated from Virginia to the Carolinas and throughout New England.

Shortly after the founding of our nation, John Chapman began his famous trek across Ohio, Indiana and Illinois planting apple seeds, thus earning him the name, Johnny Appleseed. The offspring of those trees can be found in nearly every county of the three states. Some contend that the origin of the Washington State apple crop—now the largest in the United States—can be traced to seeds brought by an English sea captain around 1820.

As the nation expanded westward, so did the migration of the apple. Of the nearly 8000 varieties of apples in the world, over 100 are cultivated for commercial purposes in the United States. Not surprisingly, the top ten best selling varieties constitute roughly 90% of the American annual harvest, which currently exceeds 220,000,000 bushels.

The apple is not finished evolving though. Relatively new varieties, those discovered within the last 50 years, include the Fuji, Braeburn, and Liberty. They join such classics as the McIntosh, Delicious, Empire, Rome, Spartan, Cortland and Granny Smith. Like much of nature, apples are a work in progress.

How Apple Cider is Made

Cider's popularity has spanned the millennia due to its crisp, refreshing character and the fact that it is relatively easy to produce. In the United States, the largest cider producing regions are New England and the Northwest.

No two great apple ciders will taste the same. They are the result of blending together different varieties of apples, each selected for particular characteristics. Some apples are chosen for their sweetness, others for their high acidity. The exact composition of the cider is where much of the craftsmanship is displayed.

After the apples have been harvested, they are carefully inspected, with flawed or unfit apples culled out of the hopper. The fruit is washed and then transferred by a conveyor to a grinder where it is pulverized into a mash, skins, seeds and all. The hopper of mash is then transferred to the cider press.

In a traditional apple press, the mash is wrapped in linen or cloth, attached to a wooden frame, then pressed, the force of which expresses the juice through the porous material. The running juice is collected in a catch pan underneath. Modern devices consist of a large cylinder of reinforced screens with an inflatable bladder inside. The mash is placed in the cylinder such that when the bladder is gradually pressurized, the mash is forced through the screens and the juice is collected.

The freshly pressed cider is sent through another set of filters to remove any fine particulate from the juice. It is important at that point to cool the cider as rapidly as possible. Fresh apple cider will keep for about two weeks if maintained at 42°F or below. Producers may add sodium benzoate to extend the life of the cider.

Sweet ciders vary greatly in their relative sweetness and degree of clarity. In addition, ciders can be still, or injected with carbon dioxide and made sparkling.

Apple Cider Hits the Big Time

Apple cider is a universally appealing drink with scores of creative alcohol-free applications. Largely its realm of use can be divided into whether it is served warm or cold.

Cider takes only about 10 minutes over low heat to warm to serving temperature. In most cases, mixologists take that opportunity to steep the warming cider with spices, such as cloves, nutmeg, cinnamon or allspice, and fruit, including orange zest or lemon peels. One mulled cider recipe calls for the addition of maple syrup and a pat of butter. Warm apple cider is a delectable treat, ideal for the holidays.

Cold apple cider makes a marvelous addition to a wide variety of drinks. It can be paired with other juices, such as raspberry, grape and cranberry.

Sparkling apple cider is a delicious way to add sweet effervescence to limeade or lemonade. It is popularly used as a base in many alcohol-free specialties.

HOT BUTTERED CHERRY CIDER

Large glass mug, heated
1 oz. cherry syrup
8 oz. apple cider
1/2 oz. fresh lemon juice
1 tsp. butter
1 tbs. brown sugar
1 dash rum syrup (non-alcoholic)
1 dash nutmeg
Step 1: Heat cherry syrup, fresh lemon juice and apple cider.
Step 2: Place butter, sugar, rum syrup and nutmeg into mug, add heated cider.
Cinnamon stick garnish

INSTANT ICED APPLE TEA

House specialty glass, ice
Build in glass
10 oz. True Crystals Spiced Apple Mix
1 1/2 tsp. instant tea granules
Stir ingredients
Lemon wedge garnish

LAST MINUTE MULLED CITRUS CIDER

Glass mugs
Step 1: Heat ingredients in large saucepan
   64 oz. apple cider
   1 oz. lemonade crystals concentrate
   2 cinnamon sticks
   1 tsp. whole cloves
   1/2 tsp. ground nutmeg
   Stir on low heat for 20 minutes or until thoroughly heated.
Step 2: Remove cinnamon sticks and cloves. Serve warm. Reheat as necessary.
Makes 8-10 servings

PINK PARADISE

House specialty glass, chilled
Pour ingredients into blender
6 oz. Martinelli's Sparkling Cider
2 oz. pineapple juice
4 oz. cranberry juice
Blend ingredients with ice
Whipped cream garnish

MARTINELLI'S GOLD MEDAL SPARKLING CIDER

Swiss-born Stephen Martinelli arrived in California in 1859, where he founded California's first commercial apple orchards and in 1868 he began producing hard cider.

Almost immediately, Martinelli's Champagne Cider began garnering acclaim, earning over 50 gold medals at competitions here and abroad. In 1916, the company perfected a process for making unfermented apple juice, and with the onset of prohibition, shifted their emphasis to the production of alcohol-free sparkling cider.

MARTINELLI'S GOLD MEDAL SPARKLING CIDER is crafted from 100% apple juice. Local growers supply the company with handpicked, tree-ripened apples, principally Newtown Pippins. All of Martinelli's juices and ciders contain no preservatives, sweeteners, additives or water. The company's 100% juices are flash-pasteurized, hot-filled into new bottles and quickly cooled to retain their natural apple flavor.

Martinelli's sparkling ciders are cold-filled and carbonated in the bottle, after which, they are slowly pasteurized and allowed to gradually cool. Pasteurization is necessary to assure purity and quality for extended shelf life without the use of preservatives.

The company's sparkling cider is the best selling in the country for good reason. The cider has pristine clarity and a light, effervescent body that develops a creamy head.

Martinelli's also makes other flavored sparklers, including Apple-Cranberry, Apple-Grape, Apple-Raspberry and Apple-Boysenberry. Each is exceptional in its own right.

TRUE CRYSTALS®
SPICED APPLE MIXER

Few drinks provide more comfort than a mug of warm, spiced cider. Between the dreamy aroma and the bakery-fresh flavors, it's a guaranteed holiday celebration in a glass. But like most things of worth, mulling spices often doesn't neatly fit into hurried preparations, or rushed circumstances that often accompanies a special occasion or busy restaurant situation.

True Crystals® has come to the rescue with the introduction of TRUE CRYSTALS® SPICED APPLE MIXER, a marvelous recreation of mulled apple cider packaged in a convenient, easy-to-use mixer. It is made from a base of fresh juice that is freeze-dried using patented technology to capture the pure, natural flavor of the fruit. Spices and sweeteners are then added. The mixer's enhanced crystals reconstitute to their natural state with the addition of water. Preparation time takes about a minute.

True Crystals® Spiced Apple Mixer is a pleasure to drink. It can be heated in a microwave or simmered in a saucepan on a stovetop. The warmth allows the mixer to open up, thereby releasing room-filling wafts of cinnamon and nutmeg. The mixer has the traditional, naturally-cloudy look of freshly pressed apple cider and a long-lasting apple and cinnamon finish.

Like the other True Crystals® products, the Spiced Apple Mixer can be used to create many different alcohol-free specialty drinks. It is especially wonderful served hot in a mug with a scoop of vanilla ice cream, blended in tall, ice cream milkshakes, or mixed with iced teas or juices. The possibilities are limitless.

QUICK APPLE PUNCH
Punch bowl, 1/2 filled with crushed ice
Build in punch bowl
32 oz. Martinelli's Sparkling Cider
16 oz. cranberry juice cocktail
1 oz. fresh lemon juice
16 oz. ginger ale
Makes 8-10 servings

SNOWY APPLE
House specialty glass, chilled
Pour ingredients into blender
1 cup apple cider
1 tbs. honey
2 cups shaved ice
Blend ingredients to consistency of snow
Maraschino cherry (snip stem) garnish

SPARKLING CRANBERRY
Champagne tulip glass, chilled
Rim glass with Franco's Lemon
    Drop Sugar
Step 1: Fill ice cube tray with cranberry
    cocktail juice and finely grated
    lemon rind. Make 24 hours before
    making drink.
Step 2: Fill glass with cranberry ice cubes
    Fill with sparkling apple cider
    Lemon wheel garnish

TROPICAL VACATION
Oversized house specialty glass, chilled
    Pour ingredients into blender
    1/2 banana, peeled
        2 oz. orange juice
        2 oz. prepared lemonade
        2 oz. cranberry juice
        2 oz. fruit punch
        1/4 cup strawberries,
            fresh or frozen
        Blend ingredients
            with ice
        Add 4 oz. sparkling
            apple cider
        Lemon, lime and
            orange wheel garnish

Chapter 10

Juices Grab Their Share of the Limelight

No other beverage seems quite as good for you as juice. We all know that juice is wholesome, but what might not be as widely known are the amazing amount of health benefits associated with drinking juice.

Fruit juice is about the best and most convenient means of replenishing the body's essential nutrients and is a great source of energy. It's estimated that drinking between 1/2 to 3/4 of a cup of juice is equivalent to eating a single piece of fruit. Unlike many processed beverages, most juices contain natural sugars—fructose and glucose. More importantly, many juices contain significant amounts of phytonutrients that have been proven to help in preventing diseases, especially heart disease.

Fruit and vegetable juices are typically high in vitamin C, beta carotene and potassium. Most are also rich in antioxidants, which are essential in mitigating the damaging affects of free radicals prevalent in the environment. If it's true that "an apple a day keeps the doctor away," then juice is like an HMO in a glass.

Not All Juices are Created Equal

Almost all juice is prepared by first removing the leaves and stems from the fruit. If nothing else is done to the juice, it may be labeled as "unfiltered," which means that the pulp, pectin and nutrients are essentially left intact.

About 98% of all fruit and vegetable juice in the United States is pasteurized, a process in which the juice is quickly heated to a specific temperature to destroy microbes and bacteria that cause spoilage and contamination. While pasteurization does extend the shelf life of the juice and makes it safer to drink, the process also reduces the amount of vitamin C and other water-soluble nutrients found in juice.

Some juice products may look like the real thing, but don't deliver where it counts, namely in the promise of good nutrition. A number of factors go into classifying the various types of juice.

Freshly Extracted Juices — These refrigerated products are typically labeled with a date of how long the juice will remain fresh and therefore safe to consume. These juices are likely to have higher levels of perishable vitamins, nutrients and enzymes. Fresh juices are rarely pasteurized.

Pure Fruit Juice — As the name would imply, products labeled as "100% Pure" or "100% Juice" contain nothing other than fruit juice. If the label doesn't identify the product as "100% Juice," then it is highly likely that the juice has been diluted with water, along with some form of high-fructose corn syrup.

Fruit Juice Nectars — By law, these products contain less than 100% juice, but more than 20% juice by volume. They usually contain between 20% and 50% fruit juice. The remainder of the nectar is comprised of water and sweeteners.

Fresh Frozen Juice — This type of product is made from freshly squeezed juice, packaged and flash-frozen without pasteurization or further processing. It is maintained frozen and should be consumed immediately upon thawing.

Juice Concentrates — After juice has been extracted from the fruit, it is pasteurized and the water content evaporated before the remaining solids are frozen. After the concentrate is thawed, water is added back to reconstitute it prior to serving.

Bottled or Canned Juices — These products are made from 100% pasteurized juice, and despite being labeled as a single variety of juice, they often contain blends of apple or white grape juice. A bottled or canned product may be labeled as a particular type of exotic juice, but in actuality contain more apple, pear, or white grape juice than that listed on the label.

Fruit Drinks, Beverages, Spritzers and Juice Cocktails — These products are diluted to contain significantly less than 100% juice, and include sweeteners and artificial flavors. Often the first ingredient listed in these beverages is water.

The Food and Drug Administration (FDA) is responsible for overseeing the labeling of juice products. All juice products must clearly state the percentage of juice they contain and every ingredient must be listed in descending order. The package must state if the juice is from concentrate or not, as well as if it has been fortified with vitamins and minerals. Be a savvy consumer and read labels on products to better understand what's being purchased.

Creative Uses for Juice

Drink making would be dull without the existence of juices. It's no wonder why they are such commonly relied on ingredients in mixology. They add color, flavor and consistency to drinks, and best of all, juices blend well.

Juice and carbonation are a natural pairing. A wide range of sparkling waters work, flavored or not. Juice can also be blended with ice cream, sorbet or sherbet. Toss in some fresh fruit and *voila*, a great tasting alcohol-free drink is ready to be christened.

APPLE FREEZE

House specialty glass, chilled
Pour ingredients into blender
1 granny smith apple, peeled and chopped
6 oz. orange juice
1 oz. Rose's Lime Juice
Blend ingredients with crushed ice
Mint sprig and cherry garnish

BIG KAHUNA

House specialty glass, chilled
Pour ingredients into blender
9 oz. Mauna La'i Paradise Passion Juice
2 oz. Coco López Cream of Coconut
1 oz. Rose's Lime Juice
Blend ingredients with ice
Orange wheel and lime wedge garnish

DANCING GUAVA

House specialty glass, chilled
Pour ingredients into blender
1/2 cup strawberries, fresh or frozen
8 oz. pineapple juice
2 oz. guava nectar
2-3 scoops vanilla frozen yogurt
Blend ingredients with ice
Pineapple wedge garnish

HONOLULU SPLASH

House specialty glass, ice
*Pour ingredients into
    iced mixing glass*
3 oz. orange juice
2 oz. fresh lemon juice
3 oz. pineapple juice
1 oz. grenadine
Shake and strain
Orange wheel and
    cherry flag garnish

ISLAND TEA

House specialty glass, ice
Build in glass
1/2 fill tropical juice blend
Near fill with cold,
    brewed tea
Splash fresh lemon juice
Orange wheel garnish

MAUNA LA'I®
PARADISE PASSION®

Mauna La'i Orchards is located high on the side of an extinct volcano on the Hawaiian island of Kauai. Its 500 square acres encompass some of the most lush and fertile land in the world. The fruit orchards of Mauna La'i—Hawaiian for tranquil mountain—are highly successful at growing a wide variety of produce, but it is renowned for its sun ripened tropical fruits. It is this fruit that is used to make MAUNA LA'I PARADISE PASSION.

This delectable drink is made from a blend of concentrated guava puree and passion fruit juice. Mauna La'i Paradise Passion contains no artificial flavors or preservatives and is pasteurized and fortified with vitamin C. It meets the American Heart Association food criteria for saturated fat and cholesterol for healthy people over the age of two.

Mauna La'i Paradise Passion is a savory taste of the islands. The blend of fruit puree and juice give it an opaque, orange hue. It has good consistency and a pleasant, tropical fruit aroma. The flavors of guava and passion fruit complement each other well, giving the drink a slightly sweet flavor and a tart, puckery finish.

The Mauna La'i line of fruit juice drinks includes three other flavors. Mauna La'i Mandarin Papaya is a delicious blend of guava, mandarin orange and papaya juice. The famed Hawaiian orchards also make Island Guava and ¡Mango Mango! juice drinks.

The Mauna La'i juices are invaluable additions to the alcohol-free mixologist's repertoire. They blend well with other, more conventional juices and imbue any concoction with a tropical appeal.

DOLE PINEAPPLE JUICE

The pineapple may never have reached its preeminence had it not been for James Dole, who in 1851, transformed 60 acres of volcanic soil on the island of Oahu into Hawaii's first successful pineapple crop. Within a few years, demand for pineapples forced the Hawaiian Pineapple Company into developing plantations on the island of Lanai. As the largest producer in the world, the Dole name is now synonymous with the pineapple.

The process involved in getting DOLE PINEAPPLE JUICE into a can is a short one. Freshly picked fruit is taken directly from the fields to a nearby cannery. There, the juice is extracted from the valued core meat of the fruit, processed and put into cans.

Dole cans 100% pure unsweetened pineapple juice, that contains no artificial flavorings, preservatives, or coloring. One sip will confirm that it is the real deal. The juice has a smooth, luxurious body and is an excellent source of vitamin C. It is incomparably balanced—not too sweet and not too tart.

Dole makes a number of products that are invaluable to alcohol-free mixology. In addition to pineapple juice, the company packages pineapple chunks, slices, cubes, crushed and bite-sized tidbits. The high quality of the fruit is evident. It has clear unblemished surfaces, bright even color and uniform shape and size.

Pineapples are a great way to add a tropical spin to even the most conventional concoction. Use it to flavor ice cream, smoothies and a wide range of frozen specialties.

PAPAYA PASSION BREEZE

House specialty glass, chilled
Pour ingredients into blender
1/2 banana, peeled
9 oz. papaya juice
1/2 cup papaya, fresh or frozen
Blend ingredients with ice
Orange wheel garnish

PEACH 'N' BERRY

House specialty glass, chilled
Pour ingredients into blender
1/2 cup blueberries, fresh or frozen
4 oz. peach nectar
6 oz. apple juice
Blend ingredients with ice
Mint sprig garnish

SQUEEZE 'O' MADRAS

House specialty glass, ice
Build in glass
1/3 fill cranberry juice
1/3 fill orange juice
2 oz. fresh lemon juice
Fill with ginger ale
Lemon wheel garnish

SWEET 'N' SOUR APPLE

House specialty glass, ice
Pour ingredients into iced mixing glass
8 oz. apple juice
2 oz. fresh lime juice
1 oz. Rose's Lime Juice
Shake and strain
Fill with club soda
Lime wheel garnish

TROPICAL COOLER

House specialty glass, chilled
Pour ingredients into blender
1/2 banana, peeled
4 oz. grapefruit juice
4 oz. Dole Pineapple Juice
2-3 scoops lemon sorbet
Blend ingredients with ice
Lemon wheel garnish

Chapter 11

Exploring America's Love Affair with Coffee

It is estimated that more than 400 billion cups of coffee are consumed each year, easily making it the world's most popular beverage. In fact, coffee is the second-most heavily traded commodity after petroleum.

Most people who rely on coffee for their morning jolt have no idea that coffee is not a bean, but rather the seed of a fruit that grows on trees. These trees are, in reality, large shrub-type plants that reach heights of 15-30 feet. Of the approximately 25 species of coffee, there are two that dominate the field—Coffea arabica and Coffea canephora, which is better known as the robusta.

By almost every measure, arabica is the coffee of choice. It is grown in over 35 countries, and flourishes in the warmth and rain of the tropics, specifically in a 25° latitude belt on both sides of the equator. The arabica coffee plant grows best in mountainous conditions between 3000 and 6000 feet, where the steep terrain and prolonged rainy season make harvesting the fruit of the arabica plants challenging and labor-intensive.

The robusta, on the other hand, is a plant that has been cultivated not to exceed 15 feet in height, a feature that greatly aids in picking the ripened fruit. It grows extremely well at sea level and doesn't require excessive amounts of rainfall. The chief commercial attribute of robusta coffee is that it is relatively inexpensive, and therefore is often used in lower priced blends. It does not, however, have the rich, robust flavor of arabica beans.

From Bud to Roasted Bean

On average, a single coffee plant will yield one to two pounds of green beans each growing season. The process by which coffee is transformed from a luscious fruit to the roasted finished product is a long and arduous one.

The secret behind the phenomenal appeal of coffee lies in the roasting process. Likewise, much of the success of a coffeehouse lies in the skill and intuition of the roastmaster. The roasting process burns off certain unwanted acids, while further developing those that provide the finished brew with taste and zestfulness.

Aside from darkening in color, the most apparent change to the bean's appearance during roasting is how much oil is allowed to rise to its surface. Up to 15% of a coffee bean is oil. The substance is essential to the appreciation of coffee because it is the oil that delivers the flavor components. The deeper the roast, the more essential oils make it to the bean's surface. For example, the deepest of the roasts is typically called a French Roast, and as such it is entirely covered with an oily, glossy sheen and the bean will appear black.

Which is the best degree of roast? That's a matter of fierce debate among coffee aficionados. A roast where the bean has attained a light mahogany color will likely have a trace of oil on the surface. The result is a light-bodied coffee with high acidity and a broad range of flavors. Conversely, dark roasted beans are covered with an oily sheen and deliver a slightly sweet, full-bodied cup of coffee with a bold, robust flavor.

While somewhat ambiguous, different names are assigned to the various degrees of roast. Depending where on the planet you are at the moment, a particular degree of roast can be called something different than you are used to. In the final analysis, what's in a name?

The lightest is called a Cinnamon Roast (a.k.a. New England and Light), principally because the color of the bean resembles the hue of cinnamon. It will not have any trace of oil on the surface, and usually produces a light-bodied coffee with a mild, delicate taste.

City Roast (a.k.a. High, Light French and Dark) creates a slightly darker color and produces no trace of oil on the surface. A Full-City Roast (a.k.a. European, Continental and Spanish) is a shade darker that may or may not produce oil on the surface of the bean. Both styles of roast have fallen somewhat out of style and are now most typically used in blends.

A Vienna Roast (a.k.a. After-Dinner and Strong) produces a dark brown color and will elicit traces of oil to the surface. These droplets will appear as minute speckles. The coffee has a medium- to full-bodied, creamy texture and is often described as having a spicy, slightly sweet or bittersweet flavor.

The two darkest roasts are the Italian and French. The Italian Roast produces dark-brown beans that are about half-covered with oil droplets, whereas with French Roast (a.k.a. Dark French, New Orleans, Neapolitan and Heavy), the beans are a glossy black and covered with an oily sheen.

Selecting Coffee Beans from a World of Choices

While coffee is cultivated and harvested in over 35 countries, buyers typically divide the world's production into three main categories based on growing region: Africa; Indonesia; and North, Central and South Americas.

Coffee is a product of its environment. It derives its characteristics from the climatic and soil conditions under which it is grown. Generally, beans cultivated in one country will be characteristically similar to those grown in a bordering country. While naturally there are exceptions, it is a useful rule of thumb.

There are those who prefer drinking coffee produced by a single variety of bean, such as 100% Colombian, Jamaican or Kona. While often a bit pricey, it is an interesting way to appreciate the distinctive qualities of a specific growing region.

The majority of commercial coffees are blends, meaning that they are comprised of beans from several different growing regions. While not as exclusive—or expensive—there are appreciable advantages to drinking a blended coffee. The intent of a blend is to marry together complimentary coffee beans such that the sum of the parts is greater than the whole. For example, a professional blender may combine beans from Central America for their delicate, rich flavor, a smaller percentage of an African variety for a splash of the exotic, and a variety from Indonesia for its substantial body.

One of the most successful and widely distributed blends is the Mocha-Java. Originally it was comprised of beans from the African country of Yemen and from the Indonesian island of Java. Today, both varieties are exceptionally expensive, so beans from neighboring countries are substituted; this with no perceived change in quality or taste profile.

Brewing World Class Coffee

The finest and most exclusive coffee beans will not salvage a poorly prepared cup of coffee. Take expensive coffee beans and grind them too coarse or too fine for your machine, and the result will be eminently disappointing. Likewise, small disasters can result from improperly storing beans and ill-advised brewing techniques.

No coffee lover need suffer through a miserable cup of Joe. To that end, the following are secrets to brewing a world class cup of coffee.

Tip #1: Properly Store Coffee Beans — An important aspect of serving a great cup of coffee is to start with fresh beans, or more accurately, to start with freshly roasted beans. Beans quickly lose their lively aroma and robust flavor, thus the need for proper storage.

Whole beans maintain their freshness better than ground coffee, so grinding them just before brewing is optimum. Do not store coffee—especially ground coffee—in a refrigerator. The ambient moisture will rob coffee of its freshness. There, even stored in a sealed container, coffee is susceptible to absorbing any food odors present in a refrigerator. Although the practice has its detractors, storing coffee in a freezer is a far better alternative.

The best container for storing coffee is opaque, airtight, resealable and made out of glass or plastic. In such a container, whole beans will remain relatively fresh for up to 10 days at room temperature. The container should be cleaned regularly as an imperceptible build-up of oil will quickly turn rank and taint the coffee.

Tip #2: Properly Grind Coffee Beans — To best appreciate the character of coffee, the best advice is to grind the beans just prior to brewing. Since there are numerous methods to brew coffee, there is no one right gauge of grind. If the grind is too fine, the water will extract an excessive amount of oil and flavors from the coffee. Likewise, finely ground coffee will clog the filter and cause minute particles of coffee to make their way to the finished cup of coffee. An excessively coarse grind allows the hot water to rapidly flow through. This will cause under-extraction and result in a bitter, flavorless cup of coffee.

The method of brewing ultimately dictates the type of grind used. The process of making espresso requires that the beans be finely ground. Nearly all of the other methods used to brew coffee rely on a slower extraction. For example, the plunger method steeps coffee grounds for two to four minutes. A coarse grind enhances the process by slowing the release of the coffee's flavor and aroma agents into the water.

Tip #3: Ensuring Water Quality — Distilled water is by definition flavorless, and to some therefore a detriment. Many tap waters are loaded with alkalines and minerals that adversely react with the essential oils in beans. The phosphates in softened water react even worse with ground coffee. Filtered drinking water, or even better, naturally balanced spring water is optimal.

Tip #4: Ensuring Proper Water Temperature — There doesn't appear to be any evidence that will lay to rest the controversy about whether hot or cold water brews a better pot of coffee. The temperature of the water initially is not a factor. However, once the brewing cycle has commenced the water temperature is of critical importance. Ideally, it should be 195-205°F. Weak or older equipment often insufficiently heats the water, resulting in under-extraction and weak, bitter coffee.

On the other end of the scale, never pour boiling water directly over coffee. Always wait a few moments before using boiling water taken directly off the burner.

Tip #5: Filter Selection — Most methods of brewing require that ground coffee be placed in either a paper or gold-plated filter. There are advantages to both. Paper filters are disposable and therefore clean and convenient. They are also inexpensive and an effective method of preventing solids from entering your coffee, although they do filter out more of the desirable oils and colloids, the minute solids that give the brew its body and mouthfeel.

Gold plated filters, on the other hand, allow more of the all-important oils and colloids to pass through to the finished brew. They are quite effective at filtering out solids, moderately priced and durable. Their chief drawback seems to be that one is left with a filter full of messy coffee grounds to deal with.

Tip #6: Using the Proper Measurements — In coffee parlance, a scoop of ground coffee is considered to be two teaspoons. How much coffee you use is obviously a huge factor in determining the quality of the finished product. As a general rule, two scoops of ground coffee and 8 ounces of water will yield a 6-ounce cup of coffee. This basic proportion can be adjusted slightly based on personal preference.

Tip #7: Keeping Brewed Coffee Hot — Prolonged exposure to direct heat will rapidly turn a pot of ideally brewed coffee into a bitter, acidic mess. This naturally raises the question—why do nearly all coffee makers come equipped with electric burners upon which the pot is meant to rest for extended periods of time? After all, every minute that the coffee sits on a burner, a chain of unwanted chemical reactions will continue to destroy and vaporize every quality about coffee that is desirable. While there appears to be no readily apparent explanation, the best advice is to immediately take the coffee off the burner as quickly as is convenient.

The most viable alternative to using the built-in burner seems to be an air-tight thermal carafe. It is designed to maintain the temperature of beverages for a considerable period of time. Filling it with hot water for a few minutes increases their efficiency. This will build up the internal temperature in the glass lining and better maintain the brewed coffee at or near the desired temperature of 185°F.

Tip #8: Keeping Coffee Equipment Clean — The equipment used to brew coffee should be cleaned regularly. There are several issues with cleanliness. The first and most compelling is mineral build-up in the machine that can diminish the effectiveness of the equipment, as well as taint the brewing process. The second concern is coffee residue affecting the process. As mentioned, coffee contains essential oils and solids that will remain in the machine. These elements will adversely affect the next pot of coffee if not dealt with.

One solution is to use a powdered commercial coffee maker cleaner. Once dissolved in water, run it through the brewing cycle and it will effectively remove residue and calcium build-up. Another approach is to use a white vinegar and water solution. It too is an effective cleaning solution.

Alcohol-Free Coffee Signature Drinks

Why leave well enough alone? To some, the sight of a steamy cup of coffee is an end in and of itself. To others, it is more of a blank canvas waiting to be altered into a singularly delicious specialty. The rich, robust flavor of coffee marries beautifully with a wide range of flavors and products. Indeed, when it comes to alcohol-free alchemy, coffee has nearly unlimited creative possibilities.

Before you skip off and start playing with the alcohol-free signature recipes that follow, take a moment to consider all of your options. In the big scheme of things, coffee can be presented piping hot, served over ice, or blended with ice or ice cream. An entirely different taste profile can be created by mixing hot cocoa into coffee, and while steamed milk is most frequently associated with cappuccino, it does wonders served atop freshly brewed coffee.

Stealing a page from the mixologist's playbook, you can pair up the flavor of coffee with ripe fruit (e.g. raspberry, banana and strawberry), nuts (e.g. hazelnut, almond, pistachio and pecan), bakery flavors (e.g. chocolate, fudge, vanilla, caramel, butterscotch and cinnamon) and citrus (e.g. orange and lemon), as well as coconut, honey, maple, mint, brown sugar, nutmeg and licorice. When it comes to making alcohol-free signature drinks, coffee is something special.

Exploring the World of Espresso

Espresso isn't a type of coffee, it refers to a brewing process. Espresso is made by forcing hot water under pressure through finely ground coffee beans. The heat and pressure cause the oils and proteins in the coffee to emulsify to produce a slightly syrupy, viscous brew. The coffee is also marvelously robust and brimming with an incomparable bittersweet flavor. Espresso is traditionally served in a demitasse, a small, 2- to 3-ounce china cup.

In Italian, the word espresso translates to 'fast,' which is an apt description of the process. Making espresso coffee requires the use of a specialized machine that heats, pressurizes and rapidly brews the coffee. It takes roughly 15-25 seconds to brew a cup of espresso with properly ground coffee.

The grinding process dramatically affects the finished espresso. Finely ground espresso produces a bitter and low-acid coffee with a well-developed 'crema,' a creamy, mustard-colored foam on top of the coffee's surface. This crema, comprised of the coffee's essential oils, is a telling indicator of a well-made cup of espresso. Conversely, with a coarse grind, less of the oils are extracted from the coffee and only a thin foam will develop. One other note, use only freshly ground coffee beans. Stale coffee produces a dull, lifeless cup of espresso.

Preparing a demitasse of espresso relies on a singular brewing process. Approximately 1/4 ounce (7 grams) of finely ground coffee is put into a heavy metal strainer. Before locking the strainer into the machine, the coffee is tapped firmly to ensure uniform extraction. Once activated, the nearly boiling water (200-205°F) is forced under pressure (1.5 atmospheres) through the packed, ground coffee, directly into a waiting demitasse.

Customarily, espresso is served with sugar and a twist of lemon on the side, the lemon being a strictly American tradition. Doctoring espresso to one's particular tastes is quite permissible.

A double espresso is prepared using twice the normal amount of water and ground coffee than in a single espresso. A short espresso, or a ristretto, is made using less water than a regular espresso, while an Americano is made using more water than is in a single espresso (typically about 4-6 ounces). A macchiato is an espresso served with frothed milk on top. A doppio espresso is a double portion of espresso made with only half the amount of water.

Making Cappuccino, Caffè Latte and Café Au Lait

Cappuccinos are typically prepared with a demitasse full of espresso coffee, and equal parts of steamed milk and frothed milk in a large cup, although this proportion may vary somewhat. The key to making a fabulous cappuccino lies in learning how to properly steam the cold milk so that it produces dense froth.

Nearly every espresso machine is equipped with a steaming nozzle. Whole milk is used to make a cappuccino, although 2% reduced fat milk works equally well. The milk is poured into a long-handled, metal vessel—preferably brass—for frothing. A container or pitcher that is wider on the bottom than at the top is considered the efficient shape for the job. The vessel should be no more than half full with milk at the beginning of the procedure.

Place the tip of the nozzle just under the surface of the milk and slowly release the steam. To prevent scalding, the pitcher should be moved continually in a slow circular motion. The milk should be frothed to approximately 135-150°F. Since it will continue to heat after the steaming process is done, the milk will optimally peak at roughly 150-170°F. When done properly, the bubbles of the frothed milk should be compact, tightly knit, and long lasting, similar to the head of a well-crafted beer.

It is important to bleed some steam through the wand for a few moments and wipe the nozzle with a towel each and every time you finish frothing milk. There are sanitation considerations, as well as the more practical concern of the milk permanently adhering to the end of the nozzle and proving almost impossible to clean at that point. In addition, the tip of the nozzle is comprised of tiny holes that regulate the flow of the steam. If not cleaned, they will become clogged and adversely affect the performance of the machine.

Once the milk is frothed, carefully pour some of the steamed milk—about 3-4 ounces—into the espresso, then spoon on the frothed milk. Again, cappuccinos are typically served in large cups and made with about equal parts of steamed and frothed milk. An appropriate garnish is a sprinkle of shaved chocolate, or a dusting of powdered cocoa, nutmeg or ground cinnamon on top of the frothed milk.

Should you field the request for a dry cappuccino, it is prepared with a larger percentage of frothed milk. A brevé cappuccino is made using half & half instead of milk. On the other hand, a skinny cappuccino is prepared with nonfat milk.

There are several exceptionally popular variations of the cappuccino, most notably the café au lait and caffè latte. The café au lait (French for 'coffee with milk') is served in an oversized cup and made with a demitasse full of espresso coffee—or strong, freshly brewed coffee—that is then highly diluted with steamed milk. The proportion of milk to coffee is a matter of personal preference, although it is often made with one part espresso to 4-8 parts steamed milk. A thin layer of frothed milk is often floated on top.

The caffè latte originated in Italy and is similar in most respects to the café au lait. In Europe the caffè latte is typically prepared using one demitasse of espresso and four parts steamed milk with no froth. In America, the drink is popularly served as one part espresso diluted by four to six parts steamed milk and one part frothed milk.

Creative Variations of the Cappuccino

One obvious twist on the cappuccino is to make it with decaf espresso, which is referred to as a 'harmless,' 'no-fun,' or 'sleeper.' Cappuccinos can be ordered as 'tall' (served in a 12-ounce cup), 'grandé' (served in a 16-ounce cup), or 'short' (served in a 6- to 8-ounce cup). A double cappuccino is made with two demitasses of espresso.

The mochaccino, which is also known as the café mocha, is a cappuccino made with either frothed chocolate milk or a healthy portion of chocolate syrup or powdered cocoa. The drink is called a Vienna cappuccino when made with equal parts of espresso, hot cocoa and whipped cream. The caramella is a cappuccino with added caramel sauce.

Both the mochaccino and caramella can be modified with a splash of Torani syrup such as mint, vanilla, or orange. Since the taste of coffee and chocolate works equally well with any and all of these three flavors, why not experiment with various syrups and create your own specialty mochaccino.

Iced cappuccinos have made it possible to sip and savor these drinks even in the heat of summer. It's made by pouring 8 ounces of cold milk and two, freshly brewed demitasses of espresso into an iced mixing glass. Shake vigorously, and then serve in an iced, 16-ounce specialty glass. Garnish the drink with whipped cream and a sprinkle of shaved chocolate.

An iced mocha or caramella is made in the same manner, the only addition being a tablespoon of chocolate or caramel syrup, respectively. Each is garnished with whipped cream, but also deserves a drizzle of chocolate or caramel syrup.

Embellishing is another way to add some pizzazz to your specialty cappuccinos. In addition to dusting the frothed milk with cinnamon, nutmeg, cocoa, vanilla, or shaved chocolate, consider crumbled brownies, nut slivers, or shredded coconut. Top the drink with some whipped cream and add a decorative swizzle, such as a cinnamon stick, candy cane, or specialty straw.

So go ahead, add a scoop of French vanilla ice cream to your cappuccino. Splash in some chocolate syrup or caramel sauce. Drop in a dollop of whipped cream and top with a crumbled chocolate chip cookie. The creative possibilities for a great cappuccino are only bounded by one's imagination.

ALMOND JOY COFFEE

House specialty glass, ice
Build in glass
1/2 oz. orgeat (almond) syrup
1/2 oz. chocolate syrup
1/2 oz. coffee syrup
1/2 oz. Coco López Cream of Coconut
2 oz. milk
Fill with cold, brewed coffee

BANANA WAKE COFFEE

Coffee mug, heated
Build in mug
1/2 oz. banana syrup
1/2 oz. coffee syrup
1/2 oz. vanilla syrup
Near fill with hot, brewed coffee
1 oz. half & half cream
Whipped cream garnish
Dust ground cinnamon

BERRYMOCHA CREAM

House specialty glass, chilled
Pour ingredients into blender
4 oz. requested berry puree
3 oz. cold espresso
2 oz. milk
2-3 scoops chocolate ice cream
Blend ingredients
Whipped cream and drizzle
    chocolate syrup garnish

BISCOTTISH DREAM COFFEE

Coffee mug, heated
Build in mug
1/2 oz. butterscotch syrup
1/2 oz. chocolate syrup
1/2 oz. coffee syrup
Near fill with hot, brewed coffee
Whipped cream and
    Biscotti cookie garnish

BITTER SWEET CAFÉ

Coffee mug, heated
Build in mug
1 oz. vanilla syrup
2-3 dashes bitters
Near fill with hot, brewed coffee
Whipped cream garnish

DECIPHERING COFFEE-SPEAK

Years ago, if you ordered a cup of coffee 'regular,' you'd get it served with cream and sugar. Now, ask for a cup of regular coffee and you'll get coffee laced with caffeine. So if you're not completely up on your 'caffè lingo,' here's a short course to get you up to speed.

Americano: an espresso diluted with more hot water

Brevé: a cappuccino made using half & half instead of milk

Café Au Lait: an espresso highly diluted with steamed milk served in large bowls

Caffè Con Panna: an espresso topped with whipped cream

Caffè Latte: an espresso highly diluted with steamed milk and little foam

Caffè Macchiato: an espresso 'stained' with a small amount of steamed milk

Caffè Mocha: an espresso mixed with hot chocolate and steamed milk

Caffè Ristretto: an espresso made more concentrated by using less water

Cappuccino: an espresso served with a layer of frothed milk

Cappuccino Chiaro: a light cappuccino made with less espresso

Cappuccino Scuro: a dark cappuccino made with more espresso

Doppio: a double portion espresso made with half the amount of water

Dry: a cappuccino made with more froth than steamed milk

Espresso: a coffee dense in body with a light, creamy head (called crema)

Half-Caf: equal parts of caffeinated and decaffeinated coffee

Mochaccino: a cappuccino made with frothed chocolate milk or cocoa

Red Eye: a cup of regular coffee with a demitasse of espresso mixed in

Skinny: a cappuccino or latte made with steamed skim milk

ILLY CAFFÈ EASY SERVING ESPRESSO (E.S.E.) SYSTEM

Founded in 1933 in Trieste, Italy, illy Caffé has evolved into one of the pre-eminent coffee companies in the world. Every day, over 2,000,000 cups of illy espresso are consumed in Italy alone, making it that country's leading brand in hotels, restaurants and bars. An additional million cups of illy espresso are sold every day worldwide, making illy a significant international concern.

One of the reasons for illy's phenomenal popularity is its EASY SERVING ESPRESSO (E.S.E.) SYSTEM, an innovative method of preparing espresso that guarantees flawless results every time with a simple, fast and clean procedure. The system consists of a single, pre-measured portion of roasted, ground and pressed espresso coffee sealed between two layers of filter paper. The coffee is 100% high grown Arabica beans blended from nine carefully selected sources. The beans are dark roasted, finely ground and then preserved using pressurized inert gases.

The illy E.S.E. system is appropriately named. The filter-encased coffee is exceptionally convenient and takes all of the guesswork out of making espresso. The system is designed to work in any commercial espresso machine, regardless of make or model, as well as many home machines specifically designed for the E.S.E. system. Since the coffee is already expertly packed, simply place the filter packet into the extraction chamber and activate the machine.

Convenience aside, the illy E.S.E. system delivers a savory demi-tasse of espresso every time. Salud!

BOYSENBERRY MOCHA FREEZE

House specialty glass, chilled
Pour ingredients into blender
1 1/2 oz. boysenberry syrup
1 oz. coffee syrup
4 oz. cold, brewed coffee
2-3 scoops chocolate ice cream
Blend ingredients
Whipped cream and drizzle
coffee syrup garnish

BUKHARIN'S COFFEE

House specialty glass, chilled
Pour ingredients into blender
1 oz. Torani Vanilla Syrup
3/4 oz. Torani Irish Cream Syrup
1/2 oz. Torani Crème de Cacao Syrup
4 oz. cold, brewed coffee
2-3 scoops vanilla ice cream
Blend ingredients
Whipped cream and
shaved chocolate garnish

CABIN MAPLE COFFEE

Coffee mug, heated
Build in mug
1 oz. coffee syrup
1/2 oz. maple syrup
Near fill with hot, brewed coffee
Whipped cream garnish

CANDY APPLE COFFEE COOLER

House specialty glass, ice
Pour ingredients into iced mixing glass
1 oz. caramel syrup
3/4 oz. apple syrup
2 oz. milk
6 oz. cold, brewed coffee
Shake and strain
Whipped cream and
drizzle caramel
syrup garnish

CAPPUCCINO, CLASSIC ORGEAT

Cappuccino cup, heated
Build in cup
1 1/2 - 3 oz. hot espresso
1/2 oz. orgeat (almond) syrup
2/3 fill with steamed milk and
   top with a layer of froth
Dust powdered cocoa or ground nutmeg

CAPPUCCINO, HAZELNUT

Cappuccino cup, heated
Build in cup
1 1/2 - 3 oz. hot espresso
1/2 oz. hazelnut syrup
2/3 fill with steamed milk and
   top with a layer of froth
Dust powdered cocoa

CAPPUCCINO, HAZELNUT CREAM

Cappuccino cup, heated
Build in cup
1 1/2 - 3 oz. hot espresso
3/4 oz. hazelnut syrup
1/2 oz. french vanilla syrup
2/3 fill with steamed milk and
   top with a layer of froth
Dust ground nutmeg

CAPPUCCINO, INTERNATIONAL DREAM

Cappuccino cup, heated
Build in cup
1 1/2 - 3 oz. hot espresso
1/2 oz. orange syrup
1/2 oz. white chocolate syrup
2/3 fill with steamed milk and
   top with a layer of froth
Sprinkle shaved chocolate

CAPPUCCINO, IRISH EXPRESS

Cappuccino cup, heated
Build in cup
1 1/2 - 3 oz. hot espresso
1/2 oz. Torani Irish Cream Syrup
2/3 fill with steamed milk and
   top with a layer of froth
Dust powdered cocoa or ground nutmeg

CAPPUCCINO, MANDARIN BUTTERFLY

Cappuccino cup, heated
Build in cup
1 1/2 - 3 oz. hot espresso
1/2 oz. Torani Mandarin Orange Syrup
1/2 oz. Torani Butter Rum Syrup
2/3 fill with steamed milk and
   top with a layer of froth
Drizzle Torani Caramel Sauce

CAPPUCCINO, RAZZLE DAZZLE DREAM

Cappuccino cup, heated
Build in cup
1 1/2 - 3 oz. hot espresso
1/2 oz. raspberry syrup
1/2 oz. chocolate syrup
2/3 fill with steamed milk and
   top with a layer of froth
Sprinkle shaved chocolate

CARAMELLA, CLASSIC

Cappuccino cup, heated
Build in cup
1 1/2 - 3 oz. hot espresso
1 oz. caramel sauce
Fill with steamed milk and
   top with a thin layer of froth
Whipped cream and drizzle
   caramel sauce garnish

CARAMELLA, CRÈME DE CARAMELLA

Cappuccino cup, heated
Build in cup
1 1/2 - 3 oz. hot espresso
1 oz. caramel sauce
1/2 oz. french vanilla syrup
Fill with steamed milk and
   top with a thin layer of froth
Whipped cream and drizzle
   caramel sauce garnish

HACIENDA LA MINITA TARRAZÚ COFFEE

The Central American country of Costa Rica is a mountainous paradise. The climate and growing conditions are textbook perfect for the cultivation of coffee, so much so that Costa Rican coffee is admired worldwide as having struck the definitive balance between acidity, sweetness and body. If you're searching for mystery, look elsewhere, but if you're looking for a great brew, try COSTA RICAN TARRAZU coffee beans grown at the Hacienda La Minita.

This spectacular coffee plantation is perched between the Tarrazu and Alumbre rivers at an elevation of 4000-5000 feet. The mountain estate covers 1200 acres, more than half of which is dedicated to the cultivation of coffee. The estate is ideally situated, such that the sun exposure gradually warms the coffee plants in the mornings and the shade of the leafy Poro trees allows them to slowly cool into the evening.

Not all of what makes Hacienda La Minita coffee great can be attributed to nature. All cultivation and harvesting is done by hand, and few plantations in the world are more adept at processing coffee than La Minita. Only 23 out of every 100 pounds of green beans that begin the process make it through the numerous quality controls.

The La Minita Tarrazu has a wafting, sweet aroma, full body, chocolaty flavor and a delicately clean after taste. It's a world class cup of coffee.

The plantation's owner, Bill McAlpin, has implemented revolutionary procedures to ensure that his coffee plants continually produce at peak production.

CARAMELLA, HAZELNUT
Cappuccino cup, heated
Build in cup
1 1/2 - 3 oz. hot espresso
1 oz. caramel sauce
1/2 oz. hazelnut syrup
Fill with steamed milk and
    top with a thin layer of froth
Whipped cream and drizzle
    caramel sauce garnish

CARAMELLA, RASPBERRY
Cappuccino cup, heated
Build in cup
1 1/2 - 3 oz. hot espresso
1 oz. caramel sauce
1/2 oz. raspberry syrup
Fill with steamed milk and
    top with a thin layer of froth
Whipped cream and drizzle
    caramel sauce garnish

CIAO BELLA DREAM CAFÉ
Coffee mug or glass, heated
Build in mug or glass
1 oz. lemon syrup
1/2 oz. coffee syrup
Near fill with hot, brewed coffee
Whipped cream garnish

CLASSY MINT COFFEE
Coffee mug, heated
Build in mug
1 oz. Torani Chocolate Mint Syrup
Near fill with hot,
    brewed coffee
Whipped cream and
powdered cocoa garnish

COFFÉ CHOCOLATTÉ
Bucket glass, ice
Build in glass
3 oz. milk
1 oz. Hershey's Syrup
1/2 oz. coffee syrup
Fill with cold,
    brewed coffee
Whipped cream
    garnish

COOL CONGO ESPRESS

House specialty glass, chilled
Pour ingredients into blender
1/2 banana, peeled
1 oz. Coco López Cream of Coconut
3 oz. cold espresso
2-3 scoops vanilla ice cream
Blend ingredients
Whipped cream and drizzle
   chocolate syrup garnish

EMANCIPATED
TOASTED ALMOND CAFÉ

Coffee mug, heated
Build in mug
3/4 oz. Torani Amaretto Syrup
3/4 oz. Torani Coffee Syrup
Near fill with hot, brewed coffee
Whipped cream and dust
   ground nutmeg garnish

HOT COCOA CAFÉ

Coffee mug, heated
Build in mug
1 oz. chocolate syrup
1/2 oz. coffee syrup
Near fill with hot, brewed coffee
1-2 oz. milk
Whipped cream and marshmallow garnish

HOT APPLE TODDY CAFÉ

Coffee mug, heated
Build in mug
3/4 oz. apple syrup
1/2 oz. coffee syrup
1/2 oz. cinnamon syrup
Near fill with hot, brewed coffee
Whipped cream and
   cinnamon stick garnish

ICED AND SPICED CAFÉ

House specialty glass, ice
Build in glass
3 oz. milk
1 oz. chocolate syrup
1/2 oz. vanilla syrup
2 pinches ground cinnamon
2 pinches ground nutmeg
2 pinches ground ginger
Fill with cold, brewed coffee

IRISH MINT KISS COFFEE

Coffee mug, heated
Build in mug
3/4 oz. Torani Irish Cream Syrup
1/2 oz. Torani Peppermint Syrup
1/2 oz. Torani Coffee Syrup
Near fill with hot, brewed coffee
Whipped cream garnish

LATTE, ALMOND ROCA®

Cappuccino cup, heated
Build in cup
1 1/2 - 3 oz. hot espresso
3/4 oz. Torani Almond Roca® Syrup
Fill with steamed milk and
   top with a thin layer of froth
Dust powdered cocoa

LATTE, CLASSIC VANILLA

Cappuccino cup, heated
Build in cup
1 1/2 - 3 oz. hot espresso
1 oz. vanilla syrup
Fill with steamed milk and
   top with a thin layer of froth
Dust ground cinnamon

LATTE, CRÈME
CARAMEL DELIGHT

Cappuccino cup, heated
Build in cup
1 1/2 - 3 oz. hot espresso
1 oz. caramel syrup
Fill with steamed milk and
   top with a thin layer of froth
Dust ground cinnamon

LATTE, GINGERBREAD

Cappuccino cup, heated
Build in cup
1 1/2 - 3 oz. hot espresso
3/4 oz. Torani Ginger Spice Syrup
1/2 oz. Torani Vanilla Syrup
Fill with steamed milk and
   top with a thin layer of froth
Dust ground cinnamon

HAWAIIAN KONA COFFEE

Hawaii is the farthest growing region from coffee's ancestral origin in the mountains of Ethiopia. The first Arabica coffee plant arrived on Oahu in 1813, making the island the last of the great coffee-producing regions to be introduced to the species. These items of interest don't diminish in the least that Hawaiian Kona has become one of the most highly sought after coffees on this or any other planet.

The cultivation of coffee on Hawaii, however, took a back seat to the sugar industry until the turn of the 20th century. Once word of its exceptional flavor and quality reached the world's brokers, Kona coffee's reputation for greatness was firmly established.

Conditions for growing coffee on the island of Hawaii are ideal. The island's three, towering volcanoes provide coffee plantations with shelter from the often fierce trade winds. The rich volcanic soil receives an average of 75 inches of rainfall annually. The sun nurtures the plants in the mornings and the clouds protect them in the afternoons, while the lush flora canopy acts like a natural hothouse retaining much needed humidity.

Today, Kona coffee is produced on more than 650 small, family-owned plantations covering about 6-8 acres. These estate farms enjoy the highest yield per acre of any coffee-growing region in the world. In 1985, the island's various coffee plantations formed the Kona Coffee Council and implemented strict quality assurance standards. So when a package of coffee says 100% Kona Coffee, trust that it contains nothing but hand-picked, great tasting Kona coffee from Hawaii Island.

LATTE, SKINNY CARAMEL
Cappuccino cup, heated
Build in cup
1 1/2 - 3 oz. hot espresso
1/2 oz. Torani Sugar Free Vanilla Syrup
1/2 oz. Torani Sugar Free Caramel Syrup
Fill with fat-free, steamed milk and
    top with a thin layer of froth
Dust ground cinnamon

LATTE, THAI
Cappuccino cup, heated
Build in cup
1 1/2 - 3 oz. hot espresso
1 oz. Coco López Cream of Coconut
2 pinches ground ginger
2 pinches ground cinnamon
Fill with steamed milk and
    top with a thin layer of froth
Dust ground cinnamon and ginger

LATTE, VANILLA BLISS
Cappuccino cup, heated
Build in cup
1 1/2 - 3 oz. hot espresso
1/2 oz. french vanilla syrup
1/2 oz. caramel syrup
Fill with steamed milk and
    top with a thin layer of froth
Dust powdered cocoa or
    ground cinnamon

LAZY BISCOTTI COFFEE
Coffee mug, heated
Build in mug
3/4 oz. Torani Chocolate Biscotti Syrup
1/2 oz. Torani Coffee Syrup
Near fill with hot, brewed coffee
Whipped cream garnish

LET IT BE CAFÉ
Coffee mug, heated
Build in mug
1/2 oz. raspberry
    syrup
1/2 oz. chocolate syrup
1/2 oz. coffee syrup
Near fill with hot,
    brewed coffee
Whipped cream garnish

©1997 Herb Kawainui Kane

LUCKY NUT COFFEE

Coffee mug, heated
Build in mug
1/2 oz. Torani Hazelnut Syrup
1/2 oz. Torani Irish Cream Syrup
1/2 oz. Torani Coffee Syrup
Near fill with hot, brewed coffee
Whipped cream and sprinkle
    shaved chocolate garnish

MOCHA, ALMOND

Cappuccino cup, heated
Build in cup
1 1/2 - 3 oz. hot espresso
1/2 oz. chocolate syrup
1/2 oz. orgeat (almond) syrup
Fill with steamed milk and
    top with a thin layer of froth
Whipped cream and dust
    powdered cocoa garnish

MOCHA, CARAMEL CREAM

Cappuccino cup, heated
Build in cup
1 1/2 - 3 oz. hot espresso
1/2 oz. chocolate syrup
1/2 oz. caramel sauce
1/2 oz. french vanilla syrup
Fill with steamed milk and
    top with a thin layer of froth
Whipped cream and drizzle
    caramel sauce garnish

MOCHA, CHOCOLATE
COVERED PEAR

Cappuccino cup, heated
Build in cup
1 1/2 - 3 oz. hot espresso
1 oz. Torani Pear Syrup
1/2 oz. Torani Chocolate Mocha Sauce
Fill with steamed milk and
    top with a thin layer of froth
Whipped cream and dust
    powdered cocoa garnish

MOCHA, PEPPERMINT PATTY

Cappuccino cup, heated
Build in cup
1 1/2 - 3 oz. hot espresso
1 oz. chocolate syrup
1/2 oz. peppermint syrup
Fill with steamed milk and
    top with a thin layer of froth
Whipped cream and dust
    powdered cocoa garnish

MOCHA, RASPBERRY

Cappuccino cup, heated
Build in cup
1 1/2 - 3 oz. hot espresso
1 oz. chocolate syrup
3/4 oz. raspberry syrup
Fill with steamed milk and
    top with a thin layer of froth
Dust powdered cocoa

NUTTY CAPPO

House specialty glass, chilled
Rim glass with sugar and cinnamon
Pour ingredients into blender
1 1/2 - 3 oz. cold espresso
3/4 oz. Torani Tiramisu Syrup
3/4 oz. Torani Coffee Syrup
2-3 scoops vanilla ice cream
Blend ingredients
Whipped cream and chopped nuts garnish

O'IRISH DREAM COFFEE

Coffee mug, heated
Build in mug
3/4 oz. Torani Irish Cream Syrup
1/2 oz. Torani Vanilla Syrup
Near fill with hot, brewed coffee
1 oz. half & half cream
Whipped cream and
    vanilla wafer garnish

PAPAMINT COFFEE

Coffee mug, heated
Build in mug
1 1/2 oz. chocolate syrup
1/8 tsp. mint extract
1-2 oz. milk
Fill with hot, brewed coffee
Whipped cream garnish

PEACHES 'N' CREAM CAFÉ

Coffee mug, heated
Build in mug
3/4 oz. peach syrup
1 tsp. honey
1/2 oz. cinnamon syrup
Near fill with hot, brewed coffee
1 oz. half & half cream
Whipped cream and sprinkle
   brown sugar garnish

PEPPERMINT
TRUFFLE COFFEE

Coffee mug, heated
Build in mug
1 oz. chocolate syrup
3/4 oz. peppermint syrup
Near fill with hot, brewed coffee
Whipped cream and sprinkle
   shaved chocolate garnish

SATISFIED MOCHA
ADDICTION COFFEE

House specialty glass, chilled
Pour ingredients into blender
2 oz. Torani Sugar Free Chocolate Syrup
3 oz. cold, decaffeinated espresso
2-3 scoops sugar- and
   fat-free vanilla ice cream
Blend ingredients with ice
Sugar- and fat-free whipped cream
   and drizzle Torani Sugar Free
   Chocolate Syrup garnish

SONSY TIMES

Coffee mug, heated
Build in mug
3/4 oz. Torani Amaretto Syrup
3/4 oz. Torani Irish Cream Syrup
1/2 fill hot, brewed coffee
Near fill with prepared hot chocolate
Whipped cream and drizzle
   Torani Hazelnut Syrup garnish

STRAWBERRY CAFÉ

House specialty glass, ice
Pour ingredients into iced mixing glass
1 oz. strawberry syrup
1/2 oz. chocolate syrup
1/2 oz. coffee syrup
2 oz. milk
6 oz. cold, brewed coffee
Shake and strain
Whipped cream and chocolate-covered
   strawberry garnish

THAI ICED CAFÉ

House specialty glass, ice
Pour ingredients into iced mixing glass
1 oz. Coco López Cream of Coconut
1/2 oz. coffee syrup
2 pinches ground ginger
2 pinches ground cinnamon
2 oz. milk
6 oz. cold, brewed coffee
Shake and strain

WINTER'S COFFEE NOG

Coffee mug, heated
Build in mug
3/4 oz. coffee syrup
2 oz. egg nog
2 pinches ground nutmeg
2 pinches ground cinnamon
Near fill with hot, brewed coffee
Whipped cream and dust
   ground nutmeg garnish

WINNIE'S MORNING
COFFEE ELIXIR

Coffee mug, heated
Build in mug
3/4 oz. coffee syrup
1 tsp. honey
Near fill with hot, brewed coffee
1 oz. half & half cream
Whipped cream and
   cinnamon stick garnish

Chapter 12

Making the Most of Cocoa Drinks

Hot cocoa is a comfort beverage. It is often the drink of choice for a relaxed Sunday morning, just before bedtime or after a late dinner. Hot cocoa is a classic American beverage—warm, satisfying and best of all, made from pure, 100% chocolate.

Hot cocoa's origins go far beyond Bosco or Ovaltine. In fact, cocoa beans were so revered by the Aztecs that they were used as money. The royalty and priests drank a warm concoction made of crushed cocoa beans and water called *chcolatl*. The Emperor Montezuma served Cortez and the Conquistadors *chcolatl* in golden goblets when the Spaniards arrived in 1519.

While Cortez lusted after the Aztec's gold and riches, he and his men had little fondness for the bitter mixture, until they surreptitiously added cane sugar. Upon his return to Spain in 1528, Cortez introduced King Charles V and his Royal Court to sweetened hot cocoa, and not surprisingly, it became the rage of the aristocracy. For centuries the Spanish held a monopoly on cocoa, until the secret of its existence leaked out.

Many countries began planting cocoa plantations in their tropical colonies. Shortly thereafter, the fame of cocoa beans spread throughout Europe. By 1657, cafés devoted exclusively to serving hot chocolate began opening in London, but it was still prohibitively expensive to the masses.

For more than a century, cocoa remained the domain of the wealthy and privileged. By the early 19th century however, steam-operated grinding machines caused prices to drop dramatically. In 1828, Dutchman Coenraad Van Houten invented a mechanized press that better extracted the highly valued cocoa butter. The innovation greatly improved the flavor of cocoa and led to large-scale manufacturing.

Cocoa Rises to World Preeminence

The cocoa tree grows only in tropical climates in a band 20 degrees north and south of the Equator. It produces kernels, or nibs, which contain up to 54% cocoa butter. When the beans are crushed, heat is used to liquefy the cocoa butter to form chocolate paste.

When dried, it is crushed and pulverized into a fine powder. Most premium producers of cocoa powder add a small amount of alkaline salts to the paste prior to drying. The salts render the powder darker, give it a more intense chocolate flavor and allow it to stay in solution longer in liquid.

One of the great features of making a cup of cocoa is that it doesn't require specialized equipment or training. Although there are many ways to make hot cocoa, the following is a typical scratch recipe.

In a saucepan over a low flame, whisk together 1/2 cup of cocoa powder, 1/3 cup sugar and 1/2 cup of water. After the powder and sugar go into solution, stir in another 1/2 cup of water and a cup of milk. Keep stirring over low to moderate heat for approximately 10 minutes, stirring from the bottom of the saucepan at a low temperature to prevent scalding. Once the mixture is hot, remove the pan from the burner and allow to cool. Serve with whipped cream, marshmallows or both for a finishing touch.

There are any number of variations on this theme. Some recipes call for the addition of vanilla extract, cloves, cinnamon, lemon juice, instant espresso powder or mint chocolate chips for flavor. Cornstarch or arrowroot can be added for thickening. Substituting brown sugar for regular granulated sugar is another creative option.

Then there's the Mayan hot cocoa recipe made famous in the movie *Chocolat*. It is made with milk, pure cocoa, unbleached flour, dark brown sugar, powdered sugar, vanilla, grated nutmeg, cloves, crumbled cinnamon and chili pepper. The drink is spicy, robust and highly aromatic. It's likely the most exotic version of hot cocoa, but may also be the most captivating.

Creating Hot Cocoa Classics

Creating great alcohol-free specialties with hot cocoa involves the least amount of creative genius and has the highest likelihood of generating a standing ovation. Chocolate is a flavor so ingrained in our psyches that creating sensational drinks with it is almost foolproof. It's about as straightforward as mixology gets.

To illustrate the point, here's how the creative mixologist's mind tends to work. Start with a 3/4 full cup of hot cocoa. At this point, the drink is almost begging for an added blast of flavor. It could be a splash of hot fudge or one of Torani's Mocha Sauces; after all, chocolate, caramel and white chocolate all complement the flavor of hot cocoa. If adding a sauce is more of a blast than desired, maybe a splash of Torani Blackberry, or Vanilla Syrup is called for.

After the identity of the cocoa base has been altered, it's time to drop in a scoop of ice cream. Shortly after splash down, the melting ice cream forms a frothy layer on the surface of the cocoa. It's a fabulous presentation. The *coup de grace* is there's a wide variety of ice cream flavors that work with the satisfying taste of hot cocoa. Have fun and experiment, there's no such thing as making a mistake with hot cocoa.

BROWN SUGAR HOT COCOA

Coffee mug, heated
Build in mug
2 tsp. brown sugar
Near fill with prepared hot cocoa
Stir to mix
Whipped cream and
    chocolate sprinkles garnish

BUTTERFINGER COCOA

Coffee mug, heated
Pour ingredients into blender
1/2 Butterfinger candy bar, crushed
Near fill with prepared hot cocoa
Blend ingredients until smooth
Whipped cream garnish
Note: Use mini food-chopper
    for crushing candy bar.

CANADIAN TOE
TOASTER COCOA

Coffee mug, heated
Build in mug
1 oz. cinnamon syrup
Near fill with prepared hot cocoa
Whipped cream garnish

CANDY CANE COCOA (1)

Coffee mug, heated
Pour ingredients into blender
1 peppermint candy cane, crushed
Near fill with prepared hot cocoa
Blend ingredients until smooth
Whipped cream garnish
Note: Use mini food-chopper
    for crushing candy cane.

CAPPUCCINO COCOA

Coffee mug, heated
Build in mug
1/2 fill with prepared hot cocoa
Near fill with prepared
    hot cappuccino
Whipped cream and dust
    powdered cocoa garnish

GODIVA CLASSIC MILK CHOCOLATE HOT COCOA

Over its 75-year history, Godiva Chocolatier company has risen to being one of the best known names in chocolate. Founded by Joseph Draps in Brussels, Belgium, the firm's renowned style entails balancing divergent aromas, flavors and texture in their chocolates.

To execute this style, Godiva relies on superior ingredients, ones appreciably different in flavor and texture. These ingredients include high-quality cocoa beans, dairy butter and heavy cream, as well as intriguing flavor components like macadamia nuts and fresh fruit fillings such as mandarin oranges.

The firm's international reputation for greatness continues to shine brightly with the introduction of GODIVA CLASSIC MILK CHOCOLATE HOT COCOA. The super-premium mix is made with little more than pure cocoa, milk chocolate and bittersweet chocolate. Fans of milk chocolate will adore this mix. Prepared with milk instead of water, the cocoa is imbued with the luxuriously rich aroma and flavor of milk chocolate. The cocoa has a full body and long finish.

Godiva makes over 100 types of chocolate, so it's no surprise that they make more than one variety of hot cocoa.

Godiva Chocolate Mocha Hot Cocoa is a sophisticated treat. It is made from a blend of pure cocoa, milk chocolate, bittersweet chocolate and premium coffee. The Chocolate Mocha mix has a delectable chocolate palate with undertones of coffee flavor. Godiva makes the combination of tastes work.

The ultra-premium line also includes Godiva Dark Chocolate Truffle Hot Cocoa. It is a blend of cocoa and bittersweet chocolate. It has a substantial body, wafting bouquet and a dark chocolate palate.

CHOCOLATE LOVERS TAKE NOTE

There may not be a more popular flavor on Earth than chocolate. One of the reasons for its supremacy and the likely reason for its universal appeal is cocoa butter. The most singular property of cocoa butter is that it melts at mouth temperature, which allows it to immediately release waves of chocolate flavor.

Chocolate is a small indulgence, one most of us deserve on an hourly basis. But what isn't widely known is that chocolate is actually better for us than previously believed.

Contrary to widespread belief, chocolate is not high in caffeine. A typical 1.4-ounce chocolate bar contains the same amount of caffeine as a cup of decaffeinated coffee. Likewise, neither chocolate nor sugar causes hyperactivity in children. Researchers claim that there isn't anything in either product to explain why kids act loony sometimes.

Chocolate has relatively little to do with promoting cavities. Because it tends to clear the mouth quickly, there is only a limited amount of time chocolate is in contact with the teeth. Also, there is no medical evidence to support the supposition that chocolate triggers migraines.

There is ample evidence, however, suggesting that chocolate has beneficial attributes. Cocoa powder and chocolate contain a relatively high amount of phenolic compounds, which possess antioxidant properties. These very compounds are beneficial in reducing the risk of coronary disease.

Finally, research suggests that chocolate may be responsible for releasing serotonin and endorphins in the brain, which make people feel relaxed and gives a sense of well-being.

So go ahead, have some chocolate and take the rest of the day off.

CHOCOLATE COVERED CHERRY COCOA STEAMER

Large snifter
Steam ingredients until well-mixed (using steaming nozzle of an espresso machine)
1 oz. chocolate syrup
1 1/2 oz. cherry syrup
8 oz. milk

CHOCOLATEY CARAMEL HOT COCOA

Coffee mug, heated
Build in mug
1/2 oz. chocolate syrup
1 oz. caramel syrup
Near fill with prepared hot cocoa
Whipped cream garnish

CREAMY COCONUT COCOA STEAMER

Large snifter
Steam ingredients until well-mixed (using steaming nozzle of an espresso machine)
1/2 oz. Torani Crème de Cacao Syrup
1/2 oz. Torani Crème Caramel Syrup
1/2 oz. Torani Coconut Syrup
1/2 oz. Torani Vanilla Syrup
8 oz. milk

CREAMY LEMON PARFAIT COCOA

Coffee mug, heated
Build in mug
1/2 oz. lemon syrup
2/3 fill with prepared hot cocoa
1 scoop lemon sherbet
Whipped cream and drizzle chocolate syrup garnish

GINGERBREAD COCOA

Coffee mug, heated
Build in mug
1 oz. Torani Ginger Spice Syrup
1/2 oz. vanilla syrup
Near fill with prepared hot cocoa
Whipped cream and drizzle chocolate syrup garnish

HAZEL'S NUTTY COCOA

Coffee mug, heated
Build in mug
1 oz. hazelnut syrup
Near fill with prepared hot cocoa
Whipped cream and dust
   powdered cocoa garnish

HOT ALMOND COCOA

Coffee Mug, heated
Build in mug
1/2 oz. Torani Amaretto Syrup
1/2 oz. Torani Almond Roca® Syrup
Near fill with prepared hot cocoa
Whipped cream and dust
   powdered cocoa garnish

HOT BANANA COCOA

Coffee mug, heated
Pour ingredients into blender
1/2 banana, peeled
1 oz. chocolate syrup
1 dash cinnamon
8 oz. prepared hot cocoa
Blend ingredients until smooth
Whipped cream garnish

MANDARIN ORANGE COCOA

Coffee mug, heated
Build in mug
1 oz. Torani Mandarin Orange Syrup
1/2 oz. chocolate syrup
Near fill with prepared hot cocoa
Whipped cream garnish

MAPLE CABIN COCOA

Coffee mug, heated
Build in mug
1 oz. maple syrup
1/2 oz. vanilla syrup
Near fill with prepared hot cocoa
Whipped cream garnish

MOCHA MINT COCOA

Coffee mug, heated
Build in mug
1 oz. coffee syrup
1/2 oz. peppermint syrup
Near fill with prepared hot cocoa
Whipped cream garnish

PEARLY WHITE
COCOA STEAMER

Large snifter
*Steam ingredients until well-mixed (using
   steaming nozzle of an espresso machine)*
2 oz. Torani Chocolate Bianco Syrup
1/2 oz. Torani Pear Syrup
8 oz. milk

RICH RASPBERRY COCOA

Coffee mug, heated
Build in mug
1 oz. raspberry syrup
1/2 oz. vanilla syrup
Near fill with prepared hot cocoa
Whipped cream garnish

STRAWBERRY SHORTCAKE
WHITE COCOA

Coffee mug, heated
Pour ingredients into blender
1 oz. strawberry puree
1/2 oz. strawberry syrup
1/2 oz. vanilla syrup
6 oz. prepared white chocolate hot cocoa
Blend ingredients until smooth
Whipped cream and drizzle
   strawberry syrup garnish

TIRAMISU COCOA

Coffee mug, heated
Build in mug
1 oz. Torani Amaretto Syrup
1 oz. chocolate syrup
Near fill with prepared hot cocoa
Whipped cream garnish

VANILLA COFFEE
WHITE COCOA

Coffee mug, heated
Build in mug
1 oz. coffee syrup
1/2 oz. vanilla syrup
Fill with prepared white
   chocolate hot cocoa
Whipped cream garnish

BATCH HOT COCOA RECIPES

CANDY CANE COCOA (2)
Medium sauce pan
4 cups milk
3, 1 oz. squares semisweet chocolate, broken into pieces
4 peppermint candy canes, crushed
Bring milk to a simmer. Add chocolate and crushed candy, whisking until smooth. Divide between mugs.
Whipped cream garnish
Makes 4 servings

STUFF IN THE KITCHEN COCOA
Microwave safe bowl
3/4 cup semi-sweet chocolate chips
10 oz. milk
1 tsp. instant coffee granules
2 pinches ground cinnamon
Dash hot chili powder
Combine ingredients in a microwave safe bowl. Heat in microwave at medium, stirring every few minutes, until well blended.
Whipped cream and dust ground cinnamon garnish
Makes 2 servings

MADE FROM SCRATCH HOT COCOA
4 coffee mugs, heated
Medium saucepan
Small bowl
1/2 cup unsweetened cocoa powder
1/4 cup sugar
4 1/2 cups milk
2-3 tbs. cold milk (for cocoa paste)
Heat the milk to a near boil in saucepan.
Mix together cocoa powder and sugar in a small bowl. Slowly mix in the 2-3 tbs. cold milk and stir until it becomes a paste. Whisk the paste into the hot milk until smooth.
Divide between mugs
Whipped cream garnish
Makes 4 servings

MAYAN HOT COCOA
4 coffee mugs, heated
Medium sauce pan, small bowl
1/2 cup powdered cocoa
1 tsp. unbleached flour
1/4 cup dark brown sugar
2-3 pinches ground nutmeg
3 cloves, crushed
1/4 tsp. chili anchos, crushed (chili peppers)
1 cinnamon stick (loosely crumbled)
4 1/2 cups milk
2-3 tbs. cold milk (for paste)
2 tsp. powdered sugar
1 tsp. vanilla
Heat the milk to a near boil in saucepan.
Sift together the cocoa powder and flour in a small bowl. Slowly mix in the 2-3 tbs. cold milk and stir until it becomes a paste. Once smooth, add the remaining spices and brown sugar, mix well. Stirring constantly, mix the paste into the hot milk until smooth.
Before serving, use a slotted spoon to scoop the cloves and cinnamon off the top and add the powdered sugar and vanilla.
Divide between mugs
Whipped cream garnish
Makes 4 servings

SPICED MEXICAN HOT COCOA
4 coffee mugs, heated
Medium sauce pan
1/3 cup unsweetened cocoa powder
1/2 cup sugar
1/4 cup water
8 whole cloves
4 cinnamon sticks
4 cups milk
1/2 cup whipping cream
Mix cocoa, water, cloves and cinnamon sticks in saucepan. Bring to a simmer, stirring constantly. Cook over low heat for 3 minutes. Slowly whisk in milk, then whipping cream, whisking until smooth. Strain, then whip mixture until frothy.
Divide between mugs
Whipped cream garnish
Makes 4 servings

Chapter 13

Tea Time is Any Time

Some 4700 years ago, the Chinese Emperor Shen Nung was boiling water when some leaves from a nearby *Camellia sinensis* plant—now known as the black tea shrub—landed in the open pot. Intrigued by the brew's aroma, the emperor drank the mixture and declared that it "gave vigor to the body, lent contentment to the mind and instilled determination of purpose." Also known as the Devine Healer, Shen Nung set out to learn more about the attributes of the plant and is largely responsible for the cultivation of tea.

Historical records suggest that tea was originally regarded mainly as a medicinal herb in China. After its introduction into Japan, tea drinking was practiced exclusively by Zen Buddhist priests, who used it to stave off drowsiness during their long periods of meditation. When the Dutch first introduced tea into Europe in the 17th century, it was shipped in small consignments and expensive, around £15 a pound in England, making it a brew reserved for the wealthy. In fact, tea was typically stored in lockable chests called caddies.

The exorbitant price of tea lead to a booming black-market trade. In England, tea was smuggled into the country through every harbor. Surging supply eventually caused prices to drop drastically and it soon became a staple in even the simplest of homes.

In 1833, the Dutch-owned East India Trading Company lost its trade monopoly with China. The seafaring countries of Britain and Portugal quickly became major importers, further dropping prices. Drinking tea was so prevalent in Great Britain that the government provided economic incentives for the commercial cultivation of tea throughout the British Empire, especially India and Ceylon (now known as Sri Lanka).

Coffee and tea emporiums sprang up throughout Europe and Great Britain. By the mid-1800s, England was consuming 15,000 metric tonnes of tea alone, making it the leading consumer of tea in the world, followed closely by the United States.

The worldwide popularity of coffee in the latter half of the 19th century brought about a drastic slump in tea production. Further staggering the tea industry was the devastation wrought by the two world wars. Tea production slowly regained momentum during the last 20 years of the last century.

Consumption of tea in the United States is skyrocketing. According to the Tea Association of the USA, annual sales in the U.S. increased from $1.8 billion in 1990 to an estimated $4.9 billion in 2001. One explanation for its surging popularity in this country are the medical studies showing that regular consumption of tea has been associated with lowering the risk of heart disease and some types of cancer. Black and green teas contain flavonoids that are highly effective antioxidants.

Tea is also lower in caffeine than coffee, something a growing number of Americans consider important. An 8-ounce cup of tea contains approximately 60% less caffeine than a typical cup of coffee. Most herbal teas don't contain any caffeine.

Looking at the Wide World of Tea

The tea plant is an evergreen shrub and a member of the Camellia family. It grows in the tropics and sub-tropical areas of the world's temperate zones, specifically in Indonesia, India, Sri Lanka and in many parts of Asia, including China. The tea plant flourishes in high altitudes and requires abundant rainfall, especially during the hot season. In the wild, the plant can grow in excess of 45 feet in height, but in cultivation it is normally kept under 6 feet, this for the practical reason of making it easier to harvest the tender shoots and top leaves.

There are four main types of tea on the world market. GREEN TEA—also known as China tea—is not allowed to ferment before it is dried. This allows the leaves to retain much of their natural taste, color and aroma. Green tea is often served as a single variety and not blended with other teas.

After harvesting, BLACK TEA leaves are allowed to ferment in their own moisture for several hours before being lightly roasted and dried. Certainly the most popular type of tea in the Western world, black teas are rich in tannins and several varieties are frequently mixed together to create now famous blends. For example, English Breakfast tea is a blend of Sri Lanka and Assam (Indian) teas, while Irish Breakfast tea is a combination of various Indian teas.

OOLONG TEA, which is also referred to as red tea, is allowed to partially ferment prior to roasting and drying. Its color falls between green and black tea. Most oolong teas have delicate, fruity flavors and floral bouquets. It is occasionally blended with black tea for a more pronounced character.

The final broad category is HERBAL TEA. Also known as infusions or tisanes, herbal teas consist of the dried flowers and leaves of plants other than *Camellia sinensis*. Herbal teas can also be made using fresh flowers, herbs, seeds, roots and bark. Some herbal teas are flavored with fruit, or essential oils and various spices. They are generally caffeine-free.

Within each of these principal categories are popular varieties of tea that merit mention.

Assam — A black tea from India with a full-body and pronounced, malty palate.

Ceylon — A black tea from Sri Lanka with a brisk, full aroma and flavor.

Darjeeling — A black tea from the Darjeeling region of India with a delicate, distinctive flavor. Darjeeling tea is prized for its quality, which is reflected in its price.

Earl Grey — A popular blend comprised of three varieties of black tea flavored with the oil of bergamot.

English Breakfast — Made from a blend of Ceylon and Assam black teas, this fabulously popular blend is robust and extremely flavorful. Often served with milk, it is often consumed throughout the day.

Gunpowder — Widely considered the highest quality of Chinese green tea, it has small, tightly rolled leaves and a subtle aroma and flavor.

Irish Breakfast — Popular around the world, Irish Breakfast is a blend of Assam black teas. It has a pronounced flavor and aroma that make it suitable for drinking all day.

Jasmine — Made from a blend of green, oolong and pouchong teas with fresh jasmine blossoms, the tea has a flowery aroma and a fresh, mild flavor.

Lapsang Souchong — A black tea grown in China, the tea has a full body and a smoky, robust flavor. The drying process relies on wood smoke, which is how the tea obtains its smoke-laced palate.

Orange Spice — A black tea with small pieces of orange peel, cinnamon and cloves. It is a popular variety of flavored tea.

Pouchong — A tea that is allowed to ferment briefly—for a briefer amount of time than oolong. It is often used in blending with black tea.

Thai — A loose, black tea flavored with star anise.

Brewing World Class Tea

Brewing tea is a relatively straightforward process. There are, however, a few pointers that if heeded will spell the difference between a marvelous cup of tea and a tepid, flavorless mess.

Tip #1: Water Quality — A cup of tea can only be as good as the water used to make it. Therefore, spring water or bottled drinking water will yield the best results. Start with cold water and bring to a rolling boil. When making green tea, the water should be just off the boil.

Tip #2: Proper Tea to Water Ratio — Typically one teaspoon of loose tea—or one teabag—is used per 6 ounces of water, although some people prefer increasing the ratio to two teaspoons (or bags) for every 6 ounces of water.

When using loose tea, fill the infuser or metal ball no more than half-full. The tea leaves will quickly expand when wet and swell to the point of impeding the free flow of water through the infuser.

Tip #3: Proper Preparation Techniques — Always pre-heat the teapot. Fill with hot water and let stand for a few minutes and drain before use. When steeping loose tea, allow to brew for 3 to 5 minutes. Since tea bags contain more finely chopped tea, it requires a shorter brewing time to attain the same degree of extraction. To prevent tea from becoming bitter, always remove the tea bags or loose tea immediately after brewing. Never allow prepared tea to boil.

Tip #4: Proper Service Techniques — Always serve tea immediately after preparation. This will ensure that it will be sufficiently hot and at its freshest. When pouring steaming hot tea into a delicate china or porcelain teacup, place a spoon in the cup to prevent cracking. After serving, place the remainder of the tea into an insulated container to enjoy later.

Chai and Bubble Teas

A veritable institution in India and neighboring countries, CHAI TEA has only recently become popular in the United States. It is a spiced, sweetened tea mixed with milk. While there are any number of variations on chai tea—rhymes with "sky"—depending on the creativity of the maker, it is typically made from black tea, a sweetener, milk and a mixture of spices referred to as the chai masala.

Some recipes of chai accentuate the flavor of the spices, others the character of the milk. The masala usually features spices such as anise, cinnamon, ginger, nutmeg, cloves and cardamom. Some chai tea recipes also call for the use of black peppercorns, bay leaves, fennel seeds, grated ginger, vanilla and star anise.

This pleasing and soothing drink is most often made with Darjeeling or Assam black tea. The array of spices are added to the tea and steeped. A mixture of milk (whole, non-fat or soy) and water are then added to taste. It can be sweetened with sugar, brown sugar, or honey.

Americans are discovering the warmth and tranquility of chai tea, an observation confirmed by the fact that it is becoming standard fare in coffeehouses across the country. Another tea-based drink on the verge of becoming a phenomenon is BUBBLE TEA.

Originated in Taiwan during the late 1980s, bubble tea is a colorful and delicious drink made with tea, milk, sweetener and "*bobas* or pearls," pea-sized balls made from tapioca starch, sweet potato flour, or sago flour. They are chewy, slightly sweet, black or white in color and quite fun to eat. The drink is then shaken in a hand-held mixing set and usually served cold, although occasionally served warm.

Bubble teas are typically served in 16-ounce plastic cups or tall glasses. The *bobas* are placed into the bottom of the glass and swirled around making for an engaging presentation. Shaking the drink not only thoroughly mixes the ingredients, it gives it a tall, frothy head. Bubble teas are served with straws sufficiently hollow to allow the *bobas* to be easily consumed.

Bubble teas can be made with black or green tea, but some recipes call for the addition of coffee, fresh fruit juice, or juice powder. They are popularly flavored with a wide array of ingredients including mango, papaya, honeydew, passionfruit and watermelon. Using flavored syrups the creative possibilities are nearly endless.

The true artistry revolves around the quality of the *bobas*. Bubble bars make their *bobas* differently. They can be sweetened and colored with brown sugar, maple syrup, or caramel. After the balls are cooked, they are rinsed and stored in sugar syrup until needed. *Bobas* should be plump, soft and ultimately a pleasure to eat. Some bubble bars warm the *bobas* in a microwave prior to serving.

The Pleasures of Iced Teas

The first World's Fair in the United States was held in St. Louis in 1904. One of the exhibitors was a tea plantation owner named Richard Blechynden. He had intended to serve fair goers samples of his hot tea, but an unexpected heat wave spoiled his plans. In an effort to salvage his investment, he offered the parched throngs glasses of brewed tea served with ice. It became an immediate hit and sparked a new American tradition.

There are three methods of preparing great iced tea. The first entails brewing tea as usual, with the exception that it is prepared using twice as much loose tea or twice as many teabags. After the brewed tea has cooled, it can be served in a tall glass filled with ice. Depending on the type of tea used, the brew may turn cloudy when poured over ice. Although this will not affect its taste, some people do not care for the appearance. To clarify the tea, add a small amount of boiling water and stir.

The second is the cold-water method. It involves using 1 1/2 times to twice the number of teabags as would usually be used for the volume of water. The tea is allowed to slowly steep in the cold water for 6 to 8 hours. Once it has attained the desired strength, the teabags are removed and the tea is ready to drink.

The sun-tea method uses the same tea-to-water ratio as the cold-water method. The water and tea are placed in a loosely sealed glass jar and set out in the direct sunlight for 2 to 4 hours. The sunlight slowly brews the tea. Once brewed, the teabags are removed and it is served over ice.

One creative option is to freeze brewed tea in ice cube trays and use the resulting cubes in glasses of iced tea. This will prevent the iced tea from becoming overly diluted. Along the same lines, freeze fruit juice in ice cube trays and drop a few cubes in a glass of iced tea for a blast of flavor.

Iced teas are often sweetened. Options include honey and brown sugar, as well as granulated sugar. A few splashes of fruit-flavored syrup also adds a delightful twist.

The same holds true for the garnish. Although a lemon wedge or sprig of mint are quite appropriate, other creative options include oranges, nectarines, limes, apples, kiwis and peaches.

R.C. BIGELOW "CONSTANT COMMENT" TEA

The family owned and operated Bigelow Tea Company began in 1945. World War II had greatly disrupted the supply of just about everything imaginable. Ruth Bigelow had grown weary of drinking the same old tea, so she went to her kitchen and blended together various black teas, then added some sweet spices and orange rinds. The resulting brew was fragrant and exceptionally delicious. The family soon became convinced that Ruth had perfected a marvelous blend and they started what has grown into one of the world's preeminent tea companies.

The blend that Ruth created in her kitchen was dubbed BIGELOW "CONSTANT COMMENT". Now more than fifty years later, "Constant Comment" is the country's best selling specialty tea. It is a balanced offering of soothing aromas and flavors. The tandem of orange zest and sweet spice are marvelous.

Bigelow is dedicated to ensuring the freshness of their wide range of teas, going well beyond how other companies preserve their products. To that end, each bag of Bigelow tea is sealed in an airtight foil packet. Individual packaging adds time, effort and expense to the production process, but the end result is undeniable.

The company's most famous blend is available in other versions, notably "Constant Comment" Green Tea, made with orange rinds, sweet spices and a blend of light, refreshing green teas. There is also a decaffeinated version, as well as one formulated specifically for brewing iced tea.

Bigelow also produces a wide range of green, herbal, flavored and iced teas, all completely in step with contemporary tastes.

ALMOND TEA COOLER
House specialty glass, chilled
Build in glass
2-3 scoops lemon sorbet
Fill with cold, brewed almond herbal tea
Lemon wheel garnish

BUBBLE TEA
House specialty glass, ice
Pour ingredients into iced mixing glass
1 1/2 oz. fruit-flavored syrup
   (apricot, cherry, cinnamon, etc.)
4 oz. cold, brewed tea, unsweetened
3 oz. milk
2 oz. cooked tapioca pearls
Shake and strain
Straw garnish (large enough for pearls)
Can be served warm

CASHMERE TEA
Large mug, heated
Build in glass
1/4 oz. vanilla syrup
1/4 oz. orgeat (almond) syrup
6 oz. hot, brewed "Constant Comment" Tea
2 oz. half & half cream
Cinnamon stick garnish

CHERRIES PUNCHED ICED TEA
House specialty glass, ice
Build in glass
3 oz. cranberry juice
3 oz. cherry soda
Fill with cold, brewed China Mist
   Blackberry Jasmine Tea
Cherry and lemon wedge garnish

CRANAPPLEY TEA
Large mug
Build in glass
1 oz. cranberry juice
1 oz. apple juice
Near fill with hot, brewed black tea
Microwave until warm
Cinnamon stick garnish

CRAZY FOR MOCHA TEA

Large mug, heated
Build in glass
1 oz. chocolate syrup
1 oz. half & half cream
Near fill with hot, brewed black tea
Whipped cream and dust
   powdered cocoa garnish

FRAMBOISE TEA FREEZE

House specialty glass, chilled
Pour ingredients into blender
1/4 cup raspberries, fresh or frozen
1/2 oz. raspberry syrup
5 oz. cold, brewed China Mist
   Blackberry Jasmine Tea
Blend ingredients with ice
Mint sprig garnish

FROZEN STRAWBERRY
TEA COOLER

House specialty glass, chilled
Pour ingredients into blender
2 oz. strawberry puree
8 oz. cold, brewed black or green tea
Blend ingredients with ice
Strawberry garnish

I LUV A GREAT
PIÑA COLADA TEA

House specialty glass, chilled
Pour ingredients into blender
2 oz. Frusia Piña Colada Smoothie Base
8 oz. cold, brewed black tea
Blend ingredients with ice
Pineapple wedge garnish

KIWI COOLER TEA

House specialty glass, chilled
Pour ingredients into blender
1 kiwi, peeled and sliced
1/2 cup melon, cubed
1/2 banana, peeled
1 tbs. honey
8 oz. cold, brewed black tea
Blend ingredients
   with ice
Kiwi slice garnish

CHINA MIST BLACKBERRY JASMINE ICED GREEN TEA

Iced tea is an American favorite, but prior to 1982, restaurants were limited in their ability to deliver a quality product to the thirsty masses. Some served powdered instants or tea brewed in coffee makers. Then the Bunn-o-matic Company introduced an iced tea machine capable of brewing three gallons of tea in 10 minutes. Unfortunately, at the time there existed no teas blended specifically for iced tea brewers, that is until the creation of the China Mist Tea Company.

From the humblest of beginnings, the China Mist Tea Company has ascended as a restaurant and hotel favorite. The firm was founded by ex-coffee brokers dedicated to developing a line of teas that would be crisp, refreshing and wouldn't turn cloudy over ice. A rather daunting objective that few, if any, tea companies at the time had achieved.

Today China Mist offers a broad range of amazingly delicious iced tea, none more creative than BLACKBERRY JASMINE ICED GREEN TEA. Introduced in 1999, the highly acclaimed tea is made from a blend of green teas flavored with blackberries and jasmine. It has a lovely yellow-green hue and a compelling, fresh floral bouquet. The tea has a light, savory flavor, and due to masterful blending, it is notably free of the grassy aftertaste typical with most green teas when served over ice.

In addition to traditional black and green iced teas, the China Mist line also includes prickly pear, black currant, mango, raspberry, passionfruit, apricot and Southern peach. They also make three aromatic and flavorful herbal teas—raspberry, peach-passion and kiwi-strawberry.

CHINA MIST
THE ICED TEA SPECIALISTS

ORANGE CRUSH TEA
House specialty glass, chilled
Pour ingredients into blender
6 oz. cold, brewed "Constant
    Comment" Tea
2-3 scoops orange sherbet
Blend ingredients with ice
Orange wheel garnish

POOH'S HONEY-APPLE TEA
Large mug, heated
Build in glass
2 oz. unsweetened apple juice or cider
1 tbs. honey
Fill with hot, brewed black tea
Lemon wheel garnish

SANGRIA TEA
Large pitcher
24 oz. cold, brewed English breakfast tea
2 cups fresh fruit, sliced
16 oz. white grape juice
2 oz. simple syrup
Combine fruit with simple syrup in large
    pitcher and mix well, add ice. Pour tea
    and juice into pitcher.
Serve in ice filled glasses
Lemon wedge garnish
Makes 6-10 servings

SKINNY VANILLA
CARAMEL TEA LATTE
Large mug, heated
Build in mug
6 oz. hot, brewed black tea
1/2 oz. Torani Sugar Free Vanilla Syrup
1/2 oz. Torani Sugar Free Caramel Syrup
3 oz. nonfat milk
Steam together syrups and milk and fill
    mug, topping with a thin layer of froth.

SWEETENED
DREAMS ICED TEA
House specialty glass, ice
Pour ingredients into iced mixing glass
2 oz. white grape juice
2 oz. apple juice
6 oz. cold, brewed chamomile tea
Shake and strain
Mint leaf garnish

TANGY LEMON PUNCH TEA
House specialty glass, ice
Rim glass with Franco's
    Lemon-Drop Sugar
Pour ingredients into iced mixing glass
3 oz. cold, brewed lemon-flavored tea
1 oz. mango juice
1 oz. orange juice
3 oz. prepared lemonade
Shake and strain
Add a generous splash of club soda
Orange and lemon wheel garnish

CHAI TEA

MASALA CHAI
Large stock pot and large pitcher
4 tsp. whole coriander
1/2 star anise
4 cinnamon sticks, broken
1 tsp. whole black peppercorns
1 tsp. allspice
1 tsp. cardamom pods
1 tsp. cloves
1 tsp. dried orange peel
1 tsp. ground ginger
1 tsp. ground nutmeg
3 qt. water
6 tea bags, black or tea blend
1 tbs. vanilla extract
Honey and milk to taste
1. Combine first eight ingredients in a
    small bowl. Using a spice mill or coffee
    grinder, coarsely grind the ingredients.
    2. Mix in ginger and nutmeg.
3. Pour water and spices into large stock
    pot. Bring to a boil, cover and simmer
    for 15 minutes.
4. Add teabags and vanilla extract and
    steep for 3-5 minutes.
5. Strain liquid into large pitcher.
6. Add honey and milk to taste or serve
    on the side for guests to add them-
    selves.
Serve hot or chilled.
Makes 3 quarts

Showcasing Your Drinks in Specialty Glassware

The secret to glassware's success lies in its elegance, transparency and presentation. Its transparency makes it an ideal vehicle for presenting alcohol-free drinks of all types. In addition, glass is an excellent insulator that helps keep cold drinks cold and warm drinks warm. The best way to make a drink look as good as it tastes is to present it in a fabulous looking glass. The glass is one of the most important elements in defining the drink's style.

A glassware type recommendation is made with each recipe. The decision as to what size of glass you will use should be based on the size of the drink. If you already have a glass that you want to serve the drink in, but it's not the right size, you can always adjust the recipe ingredients proportionately to fit your glass. Take heed that the general public anticipates receiving a larger drink when ordering an alcohol-free beverage than an alcohol-based beverage.

To determine the type of glass for your drink, consider that the capacity of the glass when filled with ice is about two or three to one (2-3/1), glass capacity/liquid with ice. Example: A 9-ounce glass will hold approximately 3-4.5 ounces of liquid when filled with cubed ice. On this page and on the following are a list of service glassware to consider for the glassware types recommended in each recipe. The references to Libbey glassware contained in the information are intended as excellent representations of the quality, style, size and shape of glasses that are available today.

Irish Coffee	Cantina Goblet	Metropolis Margarita	Bell Soda	Boot Mug
5295 ~ 8.5 oz.	5685 ~ 15 oz.	3646 ~ 10.75 oz.	535HT ~ 16 oz.	97036 ~ 1/2 liter

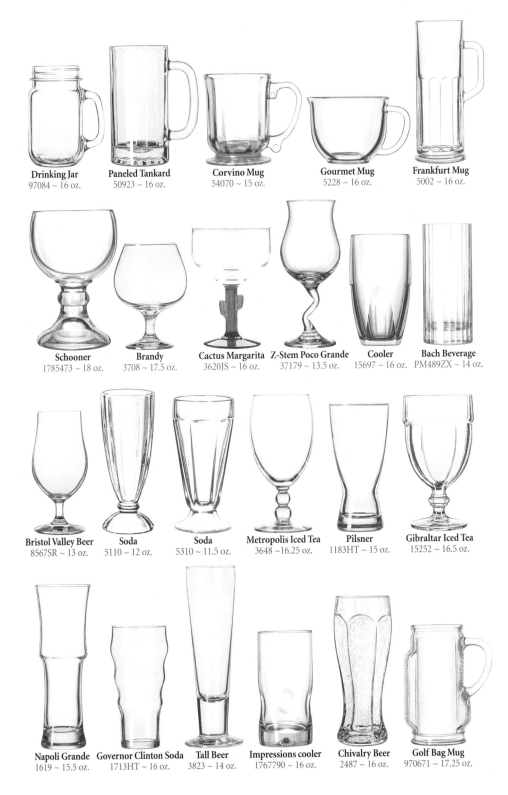

Drinking Jar
97084 ~ 16 oz.

Paneled Tankard
50923 ~ 16 oz.

Corvino Mug
54070 ~ 15 oz.

Gourmet Mug
5228 ~ 16 oz.

Frankfurt Mug
5002 ~ 16 oz.

Schooner
1785473 ~ 18 oz.

Brandy
3708 ~ 17.5 oz.

Cactus Margarita
3620JS ~ 16 oz.

Z-Stem Poco Grande
37179 ~ 13.5 oz.

Cooler
15697 ~ 16 oz.

Bach Beverage
PM489ZX ~ 14 oz.

Bristol Valley Beer
8567SR ~ 13 oz.

Soda
5110 ~ 12 oz.

Soda
5310 ~ 11.5 oz.

Metropolis Iced Tea
3648 ~16.25 oz.

Pilsner
1183HT ~ 15 oz.

Gibraltar Iced Tea
15252 ~ 16.5 oz.

Napoli Grande
1619 ~ 15.5 oz.

Governor Clinton Soda
1713HT ~ 16 oz.

Tall Beer
3823 ~ 14 oz.

Impressions cooler
1767790 ~ 16 oz.

Chivalry Beer
2487 ~ 16 oz.

Golf Bag Mug
970671 ~ 17.25 oz.

Index

ALCOHOL-FREE COCKTAILS

Candied Lemon Drop 3
Daiquiri, Bogus Banana 3
Daiquiri, Bonusberry 3
Daiquiri, Coco-Nonrum 3
Daiquiri, Faux Florida 4
Daiquiri, Faux Strawberry 4
Daiquiri, Mock Vanilla 4
Daiquiri, Placid 4
Daiquiri, Righteous Piña 5
Daiquiri, Saint Hemingway 5
Daiquiri, Unprickly Pear 5
Daiquiri, Virgin Mint 5
Faux Berry-Rita 46
Filapiña, The 6
Flying V Berry Colada 46
Healthie Zombie..6
Herba Buena 47
Holy Fuzzy Navel 6
Imitation Planter's Punch (1) 6
Imitation Planter's Punch (2) 7
Imitation Planter's Punch (3) 7
Jamocha Colada 47
Lemon Drop Tease 7
Maiden Madras..7
Make-Believe Mai Tai...8
Margarita, Angelic Melon 8
Margarita, Anita Fake 8
Margarita, Chaste Chilé 8
Margarita, Faux 45
Margarita, Faux Mama..9
Margarita, Hangover-Free 46
Margarita, Moral Mango 9
Margarita, Pristine Peach 9
Margarita, Quiet Kiss 9
Margarita, Virgin Bloody 10
Margarita, Virtuous Pink 10
Margarita, Wholesome Granny Apple..................10
Merry Framboise 10
Piña Colada, Beachy Mama 11
Piña Colada, Coolota 11
Piña Colada, Holy Cactus 11
Piña Colada, Immaculate Chocolate 11
Piña Colada, Kiddie Koala 11
Piña Colada, Make-Believe Mango 11
Piña Colada, Mockin' Toasted Almond 11
Piña Colada, Pure Coffee 11
Piña Colada, Virgin 12
Pristinely Peachie Hurricane 12
Red Velvet Sparkler..12
Sangria Punch, Berry New 12
Sangria, Sparkling New 12
Sangria Tea 98
Sangria, Virgin 12
Torani-Politan..12
Tranquil Sunset..12

ALCOHOL-FREE MARYS, CAESARS AND SANGRITAS

Angry Oyster..17
Basic Scratch Bloody Mary Mix...........................17
Bloody Blizzard...17
Bloody Boost...17
Bloody Martin 18
Bloody Olfactory 18

Bloody Olive 18
California Dreamin' Mary 18
Crushed Clam..18
Drink Your Veggies, Mary 19
Fiery Feast 19
Five-Alarm Mary 19
Free-Toe Mary 20
French Mary 20
Garlic Charm 20
Give Me a Steak, Mary 20
Italian Virgin Maria 21
Lupita With Sangrita 47
Maria Mexicana 21
Nippon Mari..21
No Blame, No Shame 21
Proud Mary 22
Pure Mango Mary 22
Sinless Cajun Mary...22
Smoky Mary 22
Swedish Mary 22
Texas Mary 22
Virgin Bloody Bull 22
Virgin Bloody Caesar 22
Wasabi Mary..22

APPLE CIDER

Harvest Punch 46
Instant Iced Apple Tea 63
Last Minute Mulled Citrus Cooler 63
Pink Paradise 63
Hermoine's Magic Potion 40
Hot Buttered Cherry Cider 63
Lemonade Sparkler 52
Merry Framboise 10
Quick Apple Punch 64
Raspberry Cider Freeze 41
Snowy Apple 64
Sangria, Sparkling New 12
Sparkling Blossom 42
Sparkling Cranberry Cider 64
Tropical Vacation 64

CAPPUCCINO, ESPRESSO AND CAFFE AU LAIT

Berrymocha Cream 77
Cappuccino, Classic Orgeat 79
Cappuccino Cocoa..87
Cappuccino, Hazelnut 79
Cappuccino, Hazelnut Cream 79
Cappuccino, International Dream.........................79
Cappuccino, Irish Express 79
Cappuccino, Mandarin Butterfly..........................79
Cappuccino, Razzle Dazzle Dream 79
Caramella, Classic...79
Caramella, Crème de Caramella 79
Caramella, Hazelnut 80
Caramella, Raspberry 80
Cool Congo Espresso 81
Latte, Almond Roca® 81
Latte, Classic Vanilla 81
Latte, Crème Caramel Delight 81
Latte, Gingerbread 81
Latte, Skinny Caramel 82
Latte, Thai 82
Latte, Vanilla Bliss...82

Mocha, Almond 83
Mocha, Caramel Cream 83
Mocha, Chocolate Covered Pear 83
Mocha, Mint 83
Mocha, Peppermint Patty 83
Nutty Cappo 83
Roca Mocha Granita 48
Satisfied Mocha Addiction Coffee 84

CHOCOLATE DRINKS
Almond Mocha Roca Milkshake 25
Boysenberry Mocha Freeze 78
Cherry Chocolate Soda 39
Chocolate Banana Smoothie 31
Chocolate Cherry Cola..........................58
Chocolate Chimp 39
Chocolate Covered Pear Shake 26
Chocolate Raspberry Delicious Shake....27
Classic Chocolate Milkshake 27
Coffé Chocolatté....................................80
Cozy Choco Belly 59
Creamy Chocolate Almond 45
Egg Cream Revisited..............................60
In The Moo'd 33
Jamoca Cocashake 27
Mel's Kid's Choco Butterscotch Shake ...41
Mel's Kid's Choco/PB/Nana Shake 41
Piña Colada, Immaculate Chocolate 11

COCOA DRINKS, HOT
Brown Sugar Hot Cocoa 87
Butterfinger Cocoa................................87
Canadian Toe Toaster Cocoa 87
Candy Cane Cocoa (1)..........................87
Candy Cane Cocoa (2)..........................90
Cappuccino Cocoa 87
Chocolate Covered Cherry Cocoa Steamer........88
Chocolatey Caramel Hot Cocoa 88
Creamy Coconut Cocoa Steamer...........88
Creamy Lemon Parfait Cocoa 88
Gingerbread Cocoa 88
Hazel's Nutty Cocoa 89
Hot Almond Cocoa 89
Hot Banana Cocoa 89
Made from Scratch Cocoa 90
Mandarin Orange Cocoa 89
Maple Cabin Cocoa 89
Mayan Hot Cocoa.................................90
Mocha Mint Cocoa................................89
Pearly White Cocoa Steamer 89
Rich Raspberry Cocoa 89
Sonsy Times Coffee 84
Spiced Mexican Hot Cocoa 90
Strawberry Shortcake White Cocoa 89
Stuff in the Kitchen Cocoa....................90
Tiramisu Cocoa 89
Vanilla Coffee White Cocoa 89

COFFEE, COLD
Almond Joy Coffee................................77
Almond Mocha Roca Milkshake 25
Boysenberry Mocha Freeze 78
Bukharin's Coffee 78
Candy Apple Coffee Cooler 78
Coffé Chocolatté....................................80
Coffee Hazelnut Float 58
Cozy Choco Belly 59
Iced and Spiced Café 81
Jamoca Cocashake 27

Jamocha Colada 47
Strawberry Café 84
Thai Iced Café.......................................84

COFFEE, HOT
Banana Wake Coffee..............................77
Biscottish Dream Coffee 77
Bitter Sweet Café...................................77
Cabin Maple Coffee 78
Ciao Bella Dream Café 80
Classy Mint Coffee 80
Emancipated Toasted Almond Café 81
Hot Apple Toddy Café 81
Hot Cocoa Café 81
Irish Mint Kiss Coffee 81
Lazy Biscotti Coffee 82
Let It Be Café 82
Lucky Nut Coffee 83
O'Irish Dream Coffee 83
Papamint Coffee 83
Peaches 'N' Cream Café 84
Peppermint Truffle Coffee 84
Sonsy Times Coffee 84
Winnie's Morning Coffee Elixir.............84
Winter's Coffee Nog 84

FROZEN YOGURT
Blue Aloha Smoothie 31
Blue-Raspberry Guilt-free Delite...........25
Chocolate Banana Smoothie 31
Fooled-Fresh Peach Freeze.....................27
Fooled-Fresh Raspberry Freeze 27
Cucumber Bliss Smoothie 32
Dancing Guava......................................67
Guava Jubilee 32
In the Moo'd 33
Kiwi-Berry Booster................................33
Mel-Ban-Straw-Bee Smoothie 34
Peachy Morning Smoothie.....................35
Piña Berry Smoothie 35
Pink Paradise Freeze..............................35
Power Plus Smoothie 36
Pure Pumpkin Smoothie 36
Strawberry Sunrise Smoothie 36
Tropical Coconut Smoothie...................36
Very Berry Apricot Delite Smoothie 36

GLASSWARE...99

**ICE CREAM DRINKS
    AND SHERBET DRINKS**
Almond Mocha Roca Milkshake 25
Apollo Blast Off 39
Apple Betty's Shake 25
Bananas Foster Shake 25
Berrymocha Cream 77
Boo-Berry Vanilla Freeze 26
Boysenberry Mocha Freeze 78
Brown Velvet Milkshake........................26
Bukharin's Coffee 78
Cherry Chocolate Soda 39
Cherry Garcia Shake..............................26
Chocolate Cherry Cola..........................58
Chocolate Chimp 39
Chocolate Covered Pear Shake 26
Chocolate Raspberry Delicious Shake....27
Classic Chocolate Mocha Shake............27
Coffee Hazelnut Float 58
Colar Polar Bear Chill 39

Cool Congo Espresso 81
Cozy Choco Belly 59
Cranberry Crazed Smoothie 32
Cranberry Orange Smoothie 32
Creamy Chocolate Almond 45
Creamy Lemon Parfait Cocoa 88
Cupid's Cloud Soda 59
Downtown Root beer...........................59
Dreamy Apple Spritzer 59
Floating Iceberg Lemonade 52
Florida Keys Float...............................60
Flying V Berry Colada 46
Fooled-Fresh Mango Shake 27
Fooled-Fresh Strawberry Shake............27
4th of July Tropical Freeze 27
Jamoca Cocashake 27
Jamocha Colada 47
Kiwi-Lime Sunrise Smoothie...............34
Mango-A-Go-Go Smoothie...................34
Mel's Kid's Choco Butterscotch Shake 41
Mel's Kid's Choco/PB/Nana Shake 41
Muddy Slide Shake 27
Nutty Cappo 83
Orange Crush Tea 98
Orange Dreamsicle Shake 28
P.B. & J. 41
Peanut Buster Swirl 28
Peter Piper Pumpkin Shaker 28
Piña Colada, Coolota 11
Piña Colada, Immaculate Chocolate 11
Piña Colada, Pure Coffee 11
Piña Coolota Milk Shake 28
Powder Puff's Sweat Bucket.................60
Purple People Eater 41
Rainbow Colada 41
Razzle Dazzle Limeade 54
Red, White and Blue Lemonade 54
Royale Framboise 48
Ruby Topaz Swirl 28
Satisfied Mocha Addiction Coffee 84
Shrek's Smoothie Snack 41
Strawberry Almond Milkshake 28
Strawberry Mango Chiller 42
Thin Mint Cookie Shake 28
Triple Decker Caramel Delite 42
Tropical Breeze Spritzer 48
Vanilla Coffee Shake 28
Worms and Dirt 42
Yoo-Hooze-Mooz-Juize 42

JUICE DRINKS
Apple Freeze 67
Big Kahuna 67
Blue Aloha Smoothie 31
Captain Marvel...................................58
Carrot Apple Smoothie 31
Cherries Punched Iced Tea...................96
Conquered Grape 58
Dancing Guava 67
Dreaming of Mangoes 45
Filapiña, The 6
4th of July Tropical Freeze 27
Healthy Zombie 6
Holy Fuzzy Navel 6
Honolulu Splash.................................67
Imitation Planter's Punch (2) 7
Island Tea 67
Kid's Cosmic Cooler............................41
Maiden Madras....................................7

Make-Believe Mai Tai............................8
Mauna Kapowni Kazaam 41
Pineapple Lemon Punch 54
Nectar of Ambrosia Smoothie 35
Orange Dreamsicle Shake 28
P.B. & J. 41
Papaya Passion Breeze 68
Peach 'N' Berry 68
Pick Me Up Citrus Freeze 35
Piña Berry Smoothie 35
Piña Colada, Virgin 12
Pink Paradise 63
Pristinely Peachie Hurricane 12
Quick Apple Punch 64
Rainbow Colada 41
Rasmanian Devil 41
Red Velvet Sparkler.............................12
Sangria Punch, Berry New 12
Sangria Tea 98
Shrek's Smoothie Snack 41
Sparkling Blossom 42
Sparkling Cranberry............................64
Squeeze 'O' Madras.............................68
Strawberry Mango Chiller 42
Sweetened Dreams Iced Tea 98
Sweet 'N' Sour Apple 68
Tropical Cooler 68
Tropical Vacation 64
Worms and Dirt 42

KIDS' SPECIALTY DRINKS
Apollo Blast Off 39
Captain Marvel...................................58
Cherry Chocolate Soda 39
Chocolate Chimp 39
Colar Polar Bear Chill 39
Downtown Root beer...........................59
Frobscottle 40
Hawaiian Fruit Freeze 40
Hermoine's Magic Potion 40
Howdja-Like-A-Little-Punch? 40
Howdy, Pardner! 40
Kid's Cosmic Cooler............................41
Mauna Kapowni Kazaam 41
Mel's Kid's Choco Butterscotch Shake 41
Mel's Kid's Choco/PB/Nana Shake 41
Orange Coconut Frost 48
P.B. & J. 41
Powder Puff's Sweat Bucket.................60
Purple People Eater 41
Rainbow Colada 41
Rasmanian Devil 41
Raspberry Cider Freeze 41
Shrek's Smoothie Snack 41
Simply Fruitalicious 42
Smurf Sweat 42
Smurfy Lemonade 54
Snowy Apple 64
Strawberry Mango Chiller 42
Strawberry Smash...............................42
Sparkling Blossom 42
Triple Decker Caramel Delite 42
Worms and Dirt 42
Yoo-Hooze-Mooz-Juize 42

LEMONADE DRINKS
Floating Iceberg Lemonade 52
Freckled Martian Lemonade 52
Frobscottle 40

Fruity Summer Slush Lemonade 52
Harvest Punch 46
Homemade Lemonade 54
Homemade Limeade 54
Indian-Style Lemonade 54
Island Guava Lemonade 52
Lemonade Sparkler 52
Lemon Drop Tease 7
Luau Lemonade 53
Mango Lemonade 53
Pineapple-Lemon Punch 54
Pomegranate Lemonade 53
Pretty in Pink Lemonade 53
Purple People Eater 41
Quick-Draw Lemonade 53
Razzle Dazzle Limeade 54
Red, White and Blue Lemonade 54
Royal Cincinnati 60
Smurf Sweat 42
Smurfy Lemonade 54
Sparkling Blossom 42
Torani-Politan...12

PUNCHES
Harvest Punch 46
Last Minute Mulled Citrus Cider 63
Masala Chai 98
Pineapple Lemon Punch 54
Quick Apple Punch 64
Sangria Punch, Berry New 12
Sangria Tea 98

SMOOTHIES
Blue Aloha Smoothie 31
Caribbean Dream Smoothie 31
Carrot Apple Smoothie 31
Chocolate Banana Smoothie 31
Cranberry Crazed Smoothie 32
Cranberry Orange Smoothie 32
Cucumber Bliss Smoothie 32
Guava Jubilee 32
Hawaii-You-To-Day? 33
In the Moo'd 33
Key Lime Cranberry Breeze Smoothie 33
Kiwi-Berry Booster Smoothie 33
Kiwi-Lime Sunrise Smoothie..........................34
Maid in a Minute Orange Smoothie 34
Mango-A-Go-Go Smoothie 34
Mel-Ban-Straw-Bee Smoothie 34
Melon Marvel Smoothie 35
Mocha Divinity Smoothie 35
Nectar of Ambrosia Smoothie 35
Papaya Pineapple Passion Fruit Smoothie 35
Peachie Morning Smoothie 35
Pick Me Up Citrus Freeze 35
Piñaberry Smoothie 35
Pink Paradise Freeze 35
Power Plus Smoothie 36
Pure Pumpkin Smoothie 36
Spiced Peach Freeze Smoothie........................36
Strawberry Sunrise Smoothie 36
Time for a Run Breakfast Smoothie 36
Tropical Coconut Smoothie............................36
Very Berry Apricot Delite Smoothie 36
Zesty Cantaloupe Smoothie...........................36

SODA DRINKS
Captain Marvel..58
Cherries Punched Iced Tea............................96

Chocolate Cherry Cola.................................58
Coffee Hazelnut Float 58
Colar Polar Bear Chill 39
Conquered Grape 58
Cozy Choco Belly 59
Cupid's Cloud Soda 59
Downtown Root Beer..................................59
Dreamy Apple Spritzer 59
Egg Cream Revisited...................................60
Floating Iceberg Lemonade 52
Florida Keys Float......................................60
Harvest Punch 46
Howdja-Like-A-Little-Punch? 40
Howdy, Pardner! 40
Italian Cream Soda 60
Lemon Cream Soda 60
Mauna Kapowni Kazaam 41
Miss Georgia Mist 60
Pink Manifesto 60
Powder Puff's Sweat Bucket...........................60
Quick Apple Punch 64
Royal Cincinnati 60
Seaweed Grog 60
Sicilian Splash 60
Smurf Sweat 42
Squeeze 'O' Madras....................................68
Strawberry Smash......................................42
Sweet 'N' Sour Apple 68
Tranquil Sunset 12
Yoo-Hooze-Mooz-Juize 42

SORBET DRINKS
Almond Tea Cooler 96
Caribbean Dream Smoothie 31
Cucumber Bliss Smoothie 32
Dreaming of Mangoes 45
Fats-No Domino 45
Margarita, Wholesome Granny Apple................10
Orange Dreamsicle Shake 28
Raspberry Cider Freeze 41
Tropical Cooler 68

TEA DRINKS, COLD
Bubble Tea..96
Cherries Punched Iced Tea............................96
Faux Berry-Rita 46
Framboise Tea Freeze 97
Frozen Strawberry Tea Cooler 97
Harvest Punch 46
Herba Buena 47
I Luv a Great Piña Colada Tea 97
Instant Iced Apple Tea 63
Island Tea 67
Kiwi Cooler Tea 97
Margarita, Faux 45
Masala Chai 98
Orange Crush Tea 98
Sangria Tea 98
Sweetened Dreams Iced Tea 98
Tangy Lemon Punch Tea 98

TEA DRINKS, HOT
Cashmere Tea 96
Cranappley Tea 96
Crazy for Mocha Tea 97
Masala Chai 98
Pooh's Honey-Apple Tea 98
Skinny Vanilla Caramel Tea Latte 98

Resources

Beverage Specialties, Ltd.
196 Newton Street
Fredonia, NY 14063
Tel 800.828.8915
www.majorpeters.com
Major Peters' Bloody Mary Mixes,
Major Peters' Cocktail Mixes

China Mist
7435 East Tierra Buena Lane
Scottsdale, AZ 85260
Tel 480.998.8807
www.chinamist.com
China Mist Teas

Coco López, Inc.
8000 Governors Square Boulevard
Suite #102
Miami Lakes, FL 33016
Tel 305.820.9095
www.cocolopez.com
Coco López Cream of Coconut

Crystals International Inc.
600 West M.L. King, Jr. Boulevard
Plant City, FL 33563
Tel 800.863.2169
www.crystalsinternationalfoods.com
www.truecrystals.com
True Crystals® Lemonade/Limeade
Mixers, True Crystals® Margarita Mixer,
True Crystals® Sangria Mixer, True
Crystals® Vanilla/Orange Crème Mixers,
True Crystals® Cocktail Mixers, True
Crystals® Apple Cider Mixer and
Crystals International Foods™ Vanilla
Smoothie Base

Dole Food Company, Inc.
One Dole Drive
Westlake Village, CA 91362
Tel 800.723.9868
www.dole.com
Dole Pineapple Juice

Franco's Cocktail Mixes
121 Southwest 5th Court
Pompano Beach, FL 33060
Tel 800.782.4508
www.francoscocktailmixes.com
francocktl@aol.com
Franco's Colored Salts and Sugars

Freshies Food Corporation
4860 Broadway
Denver, CO 80216
Tel 303.382.1805
www.freshies.com
Freshies Bloody Mary Mixes,
Freshies Margarita Mixes

Godiva Chocolatier, Inc.
355 Lexington Avenue, Floor 16
New York, NY 10017
Tel 212.984.5900
www.godiva.com
Godiva Hot Cocoas

illycaffè North America, Inc.
200 Clearbrook Road
Elmsford, New York 10523
Tel 800-USA-ILLY (800.872.4559)
www.illyusa.com
Easy Serving Espresso (E.S.E.) System

Island Oasis
141 Norfolk Street
Walpole, MA 02081
Tel 508.660.1176
www.islandoasis.com
Island Oasis Smoothies

Jones Soda Company
234 9th Avenue North
Seattle, WA 98109
Tel 206.624.3357
www.jonessoda.com
Jones Specialty Sodas

Kona Coffee Council
P O Box 2077
Kealakekua, HI 96750
www.kona-coffee-council.com
Kona Coffees

La Minita Coffee
P.O. Box 66
Bar Harbor, ME 04609
Tel 207.244.7910
www.laminita.com
  La Minita Tarrazu Coffee

Libbey Inc.
300 Madison Avenue
Toledo, OH 43604
Tel 419.325.2100
www.libbey.com
  Libbey Glassware

Lyons Magnus
1636 South 2nd Street
Fresno, CA 93702
Tel 800.546.0853
www.lyonsmagnus.com
www.mauifrozendrinks.com
  Maui Frozen Fruit Smoothies

McIlhenny Company
601 Poydras
Suite #1815
New Orleans, LA 70130
Tel 504.523.7370
www.tabasco.com
  TABASCO® Bloody Mary Mixes

Mott's North America
6 High Ridge Park
Stamford, CT 06905
Tel 800.299.0119
www.motts.com
  *Clamato® Tomato Cocktail, Fruit Juicy
  Red Hawaiian Punch®, Margaritaville®
  Margarita Mix, Mauna La'i® Juices,
  Mr & Mrs T® Bloody Mary Mix, Mr &
  Mrs T® Mixers, ReaLemon®/ReaLime®,
  Rose's® Sweetened Lime Juice/Rose's®
  Grenadine, Yoo-hoo® Chocolate Drink*

Perfect Puree of Napa Valley
975 Vintage Avenue
Suite B
St Helena, CA 94574
Tel 800.556.3707
www.perfectpuree.com
  Prickly Pear Cactus Fruit Puree

Perkins Foods
631 North Santa Cruz Avenue
Los Gatos, CA 95030
Tel 408.378.5557
www.perkinsfoods.com
drswami@aol.com
  *Dr. Swami and Bone Daddy's
  Gourmet Marga. ia Mix*

R.C. Bigelow, Inc.
Mail Order Division
P. O. Box 326204
Fairfield, CT 06432
Tel 888.244.3569
www.bigelowtea.com
  Bigelow Teas

R. Torre & Co./Torani
233 East Harris Avenue
So. San Francisco, CA 94080
Tel 800.775.1925 or 650.875.1200
www.torani.com
  *Torani Flavoring Syrups,
  Torani Frusia Smoothie Bases,
  Torani Mocha Flavoring Sauces*

Shasta Beverages, Inc.
26901 Industrial Boulevard
Hayward, CA 94545
Tel 510.783.3200
www.shastapop.com
  Shasta Soda

S. Martinelli & Co.
P.O. Box 1868
Watsonville, CA 950
Tel 800.662.1868
www.martinellis.com
  Martinelli's Gold Medal Sparkling Cider

Zoo Piks, International
3809 Pipestone Road
Dallas, TX 75212
Tel 800.321.7667
www.zoopiks.com
  Drink Stirs and Piks